Martha Frances

P9-DEN-300

HOLY
HOSPITALITY

HOLY HOSPITALITY

WORSHIP AND THE BAPTISMAL COVENANT

A Practical Guide for Congregations

CLAYTON L. MORRIS

CHURCH PUBLISHING
New York

Copyright © 2005 by Clayton L. Morris

All rights reserved.

A catalog record for this book is available from
the Library of Congress.

ISBN 0-89869-359-4

Church Publishing Incorporated
445 Fifth Avenue
New York, NY 10016
www.churchpublishing.org

5 4 3 2 1

Contents

Contents

Part Three
LITURGICAL MINISTRIES:
SETTING GOD'S TABLE FOR THE FEAST OF THE KINGDOM

Contents

Contents

Part Four
PROGRAMMATIC STRATEGIES: CHANGING THE RULES IN COMMUNITY

An Introductory Word

This writer is a priest of the Episcopal Church with forty years' experience as a liturgical planner. That history makes it almost impossible not to write from the particular perspective forged by that experience over time. Having said that, I hope that the thoughts gathered here have broad application for any Christian community whose primary weekly experience of worship is a eucharistic rite.

If the flavor of the text is occasionally jarring, seeming too Anglican in its ethos, I hope I can be forgiven, since the intent is to welcome all who find the liturgical habit of feeding and being fed central to the worship of the Christian faith.

Acknowledgments

Thanks to Massey Hamilton Shepherd Jr., my liturgics professor, and his fellow founders of Associated Parishes for Liturgy and Mission, whose vision shaped the 1979 Book of Common Prayer and thus provided a foundation for my theological and liturgical journey.

To Bill, Molly, Charles, Joe Morris, Juan, Joe, and a host of other colleagues with whom I've had the pleasure of working toward a liturgical expression of the church's mission in the world.

To Alex, Andrew, Ricardo, and Frank, friends who listened to my theological ranting and advised me on the manuscript.

And to my family: Mary, Andrea, Jon, Dan, Gena, Amanda, Danielle, and Kaden, who put up with me.

Preface

Why worship?

THE RELATIONSHIP BETWEEN WORSHIP AND
CHRISTIAN SERVICE

This is a book about <u>welcoming</u>, about <u>hospitality as a way</u>
<u>of life.</u> The theme of hospitality is central because we live
in a world in which the church cannot sustain itself from
within. If, as followers of Christ, we expect to continue to
gather around Christ's Holy Table as a way of expressing our
commitment to the ministry to which Christ calls us, we
must <u>welcome the newcomer,</u> <u>proclaiming the good news</u>
<u>to the huge population yet untouched</u> by its promise of life
<u>eternal</u>.

A book on worship presupposes the <u>necessity of worship</u>.
Those who have been long-term churchgoers probably take
weekly and even daily worship for granted. It's just something we do. But at the beginning of a consideration of
liturgical strategies, it is probably useful to ask the obvious
question: *Why do we worship?*

In conversations about a rationale for worship, one hears
contrasting answers. Some will say that congregations come
to liturgy in order to hear and be convinced by the call to
ministry. This point of view asserts that the purpose of the
church is to create that conviction and that the worshiper's
response is mission in, to, and for the world.

Others will say that God's mission is to urge people toward acts of charity in, to, and for the world, and that as people encounter the world and its needs for nourishment and healing, they are drawn into communities committed to the life of prayer. Worship, from this point of view, is the response faithful people make to their urge toward ministry. They come to church to find a community of support with whom they can maintain the courage to be Christ's Body in the world. Everyone who worships regularly surely comes, to some degree, out of an urge to quench spiritual thirst. But God's hope is that this spiritual thirst is always assuaged in the context of the church's work in the world.

Whatever the motivation people feel as they participate in the liturgical life of a Christian community, the important thing is the absolute necessity of maintaining a constant connection between the prayer life of a community and its commitment to active ministry. The focus of the life of the community must be a recognition that God's mission is to restore the wholeness of creation. And further, it is essential that the community know that their life in the world of everyday existence is the *only* agency through which that mission can be realized. When the focus of the community and its members is entirely in the arena of spirituality and personal piety, it is easy for the urge toward ministry to be lost. But to take the opposing view, if the focus of life in the community is on mission and ministry in and to the world, it is hard to avoid articulating and reflecting on experience in spiritual terms.

Human consciousness is inherently spiritual. As beings capable of imagining the end of life, humans are capable of imagining life after death and a variety of approaches to life in the moment. We see only too clearly how the effect of variant approaches to life in the here-and-now and life as an eternal state of being react and interact in the human community. Yes, worship and spirituality are inevitably part of human life. To reiterate: it is essential for the church to maintain a balanced relationship between spirituality and ministry. And more to the point, it is essential that the world's need for restoration to wholeness hold a place of privilege in the life of the community

God's mission in, for, and to the world is the restoration of wholeness. That means that people must be fed, clothed, housed, and healthy in order to participate in the life of abundance that God promises.

Attention to hospitality is an essential ingredient in any approach to this ministry. As the church practices inviting the newcomer into community, as the members of the congregation feed one another and hear God's word and each other's stories, everyone gets a glimpse of what it means to be whole and living in community. And so, the congregation explores avenues of hospitality as a way of opening communities to the possibility of a new or renewed sense of what it means to be Christ's Body, ministering in the world.

It probably should be observed that attention to the newcomer in church is not a perspective easy for Episcopalians to maintain. In earlier times, one's attention during a service of worship was focused on the activity playing out east of the altar rail. We were taught to save whatever interaction we intended with fellow worshipers for the coffee hour or, perhaps, the sidewalk. One hears criticism of liturgical leaders who pepper the service with announcements, explanations of what will come next, or comments to make the stranger feel welcome. To be clear: hospitality to the visitor, newcomer, or stranger is essential to the life and future of the church! The annoyance seasoned members of the community might experience as the newcomer is welcomed is less important than the fact that the newcomer is welcomed.

With this vision of hospitality in mind, let us turn to the question of how the newcomer is integrated into the life of the community. A potent vehicle for the initiation of the adult newcomer that reflects an understanding of the need for hospitality is Adult Catechumenal Process. The encounter between an inquiring adult with the urge to engage in a ministry of social justice and the congregation the seeker hopes will provide a venue in which that ministry might be realized is more than adequately described in other places. For this inquiry, the important point to be made is that the church's ministry, of necessity, is characterized by an encounter of the Christian community with the world at large. The congregation willing to risk a conversation about ministry with the stranger who wanders in to inquire will be transformed in the process. "Is this a community that can support me as I find some way to feed the homeless in the neighborhood?" This is a question that can be easily teased out of the language of the baptismal covenant in the Book of Common Prayer and is reflected clearly in the description of the church's ministry contained in the Catechism. But it is not always the first question to be asked during a typical Sunday morning liturgy.

The pattern of Adult Catechumenal Process outlined in the Episcopal Church's *Book of Occasional Services* and similar books from other denominations is a pattern of regular eucharistic worship, daily prayer, regular Bible study, and sustained involvement with ministry in the community.[1] The process is engaged by inquirers, their sponsors in the community, the catechists who facilitate the process, and the hospitality team who make sure that the whole enterprise articulates the reality of God's abundance. The inquiry plays out over the course of a significant period of time, and its progress is marked weekly in the Sunday eucharist.

Much has been said over the last twenty years or so about the question of how the church repopulates itself. In earlier times, children were introduced to the life of the Christian community as a matter of course. Most took a sabbatical during their high school and college years, but marriage and children brought them back into the community. This pattern, in which the affiliation with church is part of what is handed down from parent to child, has nearly disappeared. Denominational loyalty is far less potent than it used to be. Church affiliation is no longer a cultural expectation in most communities. The general population includes hoards of people whose life experience is utterly devoid of religious experience.

This current cultural circumstance presents a serious challenge for the church. Attempts to restore the cultural expectation of a religious component in the life of a community will fail. If the nascent urge toward compassion that God places in every human soul is seen as a resource that can be harvested to forge a new and renewed sense of how the church is in the world, transformation and growth will

---

1. See Daniel T. Benedict Jr., *Come to the Waters: Baptism and Our Ministry of Welcoming Seekers and Making Disciples* (Nashville: Disciples Resources, 1994); *Welcome to Christ: A Lutheran Introduction to the Catechumenate* (Minneapolis: Augsburg Fortress, 1997); John W. B. Hill, *Making Disciples: Serving Those Who Are Entering the Christian Life* (Toronto: The Hoskin Groups, 1991).

result. Some scheme for Christian formation that takes the unchurched seeker into account is essential.

It is with that in mind that this inquiry focuses on hospitality. Human life longs for wholeness. Life demands food, shelter, companionship, and purpose. The gospel proclaims the good news that those demands have already been met. If the church intends to involve itself in the drive that all God's creatures experience, the best advertisement is welcome.

Why this book?
LEADING WORSHIP IN THE CONTEXT OF THE BAPTISMAL COVENANT

As one example of the reformation of congregational life that characterized the work done in most Christian denominations during the last century, the framers of the 1979 Book of Common Prayer began their work when they realized that the patterns of worship in place in the early part of the twentieth century no longer met the needs of the emerging culture. These clergy, struggling to make sense of parish life and eager to find a renewed connection between the liturgical life of the church and its ministry to the world, discerned that a renewed focus on the eucharist as the primary, weekly celebration in the community, and situating the baptismal rite within the eucharistic celebration, would provide the church with a renewed sense of its place in the world. They realized, as well, that the weekly eucharist was an event in the life of the community that needed to gather the entire community, regardless of age.

The twentieth century was a time of rapid cultural change. On every front, broadly held cultural habits and assumptions were being challenged, altered, and sometimes abandoned. Perhaps it is fair to note an analogy between the experience of the drafters of the 1979 Book of Common Prayer and the experience of church in relation to culture later in the century. In the 1930s and 1940s, priests serving congregations came to the conclusion that the church of the twentieth century could not function with a sixteenth-century worldview. Likewise, in the post–World War II years, the church began to realize that old patterns of behavior and long-standing cultural assumptions were eroding to the point that new ways of thinking, behaving, and, in fact, believing were in order.

In the 1950s, the church thrived in the context of old assumptions. In the Episcopal Church, people expected to have a denominational affiliation and considered weekly worship a part of their civic responsibility. Children were expected to attend Sunday school. Household budgets included a gift to the local congregation

It has often been noted that the church adopted the 1979 Book of Common Prayer without giving much attention to its radical commitment to social justice. Liturgical habit is difficult to change. And so, many of the patterns that characterized worship in the early decades of the twentieth century were simply rolled over into the use of the new book, even though its rites and expectations ached for a different model.

William Seth Adams addresses these issues in his book *Shaped by Images: One Who Presides.*[2] This book presents a model for the eucharistic president as one who facilitates the eucharistic celebration of the entire congregation. This model, which erases the hierarchical assumptions that

2. William Seth Adams, *Shaped by Images: One Who Presides* (New York: Church Publishing, 1995).

characterized images of congregations at the beginning of the twentieth century, presents an image in which the baptismal responsibility of all Christians to be ministers on behalf of the church to the world is in the place of privilege.

The model of the presider in the liturgy is important, but a baptismal perspective will be convincingly articulated in the life of a congregation only when all the liturgical ministries are expressed in this mode. Thus, this conversation about the style in which various liturgical roles are carried out is offered.

A *word about terminology:* If the purpose of this book is to create a renewed focus on ministry in, to, and for the life of the world, it is dangerous to talk about liturgy as ministry. At the same time, people who give their time, energy, and devotion to the roles that are the subject of this book give generously and sometimes sacrificially in order that the weekly round of worship in a congregation is engaged with purpose and dignity. Thus, the reader must bear in mind that a liturgical ministry, essential for the life of the community, is an important commitment but one that is distinct from the essential call to which all Christians are invited, that is, the call to

. . . restore all people to unity with God and each other in Christ.[3]

---

3. The Catechism, Book of Common Prayer, 855.

Part One

The Church and Its Ministry

Restoring the Wholeness of God's Creation

The feeding of the five thousand

A STORY ABOUT HOSPITALITY

All four gospels tell the story of the miraculous feeding of a huge crowd. Jesus and his friends wanted to get away for a while. They walked into the countryside, and a crowd followed them. As the story goes, five thousand men, with an undisclosed number of women and children, followed Jesus and the disciples, hoping to hear Jesus teach. As the day wore on, it was time for something to eat. There was nothing at hand: no caterer, no fast-food stands. "What do we have?" Jesus asked. "Five loaves and two fish," one of the disciples answered. Jesus took a loaf, broke it, and passed the pieces to people nearby. He made the same gesture with the fish. When the meal was over, baskets of leftovers remained.

What happened? What does it mean?

The simplest exegesis is probably the best. Of course, there were no restaurants in the countryside. But there was lots of food in the city. It would have been almost second nature for folks intending to be in the countryside for the day to grab a little something to take along. One imagines that everyone — at least the adults — would have planned for the inevitability of midday hunger. And so, when Jesus made the initial gesture of hospitality, passing to those nearby the food he had in hand, others reached into their satchels to dig out what they had brought along. It's not hard to imagine why there was so much left over. We humans like to eat. If we're going to err, we're likely to grab too much, not too little.

The feeding of the five thousand is a story about holy hospitality. Jesus does what he always does. He uses the occasion to make a point about the way life is supposed to be. People are to be fed. Life is like a great banquet. Even in the wilderness, with no visible food supply in sight, the crowd is satisfied and there is an abundance of food left over. Alleluia!

The image of abundant food is essential to an understanding of Christian ministry. It's all about feeding and being fed. At any moment in the day, some of us can feed. Some of us need food. The church is about making connections between those who have food and those who need it. The story of the five thousand is a reminder that it isn't all that complicated.

The baptismal promises
THE CHURCH'S COMMITMENT TO CHRISTIAN SERVICE

The 1979 Book of Common Prayer distinguishes itself from its predecessor largely in its insistence on a baptismal ecclesiology. That is, the book assumes that the ministry of the church is carried out in the world by its baptized members. Clergy are set apart to facilitate the ministry of the baptized. They are not set apart to minister on behalf of the congregation, nor are they set apart to provide the members of a congregation with a sense of spiritual well-being. This is not to say that clergy have no responsibility for pastoral care, but simply to state as clearly as possible that the church's commitment to service is the work of the people.

Notice these details from the Prayer Book:

From the Catechism...

The Church

Q. What is the mission of the Church?

A. The mission of the Church is to restore all people to unity with God and each other in Christ.

Q. How does the Church pursue its mission?

A. The Church pursues its mission as it prays and worships, proclaims the Gospel, and promotes justice, peace, and love.

Q. Through whom does the Church carry out its mission?

A. The Church carries out its mission through the ministry of all its members.

The Ministry

Q. Who are the ministers of the Church?

A. The ministers of the Church are lay persons, bishops, priests, and deacons.

Q. What is the ministry of the laity?

A. The ministry of lay persons is to represent Christ and his Church; to bear witness to him wherever they may be; and, according to the gifts given them, to carry on Christ's work of reconciliation in the world; and to take their place in the life, worship, and governance of the Church.

Q. What is the ministry of a bishop?

A. The ministry of a bishop is to represent Christ and his Church, particularly as apostle, chief priest, and pastor of a diocese; to guard the faith, unity, and discipline of the whole Church; to proclaim the Word of God; to act in Christ's name for the reconciliation of the world and the building up of the Church; and to ordain others to continue Christ's ministry.

Q. What is the ministry of a priest or presbyter?

A. The ministry of a priest is to represent Christ and his Church, particularly as pastor to the people; to share with the bishop in the overseeing of the Church; to proclaim the Gospel; to administer the sacraments; and to bless and declare pardon in the name of God.

Q. What is the ministry of a deacon?

A. The ministry of a deacon is to represent Christ and his Church, particularly as a servant of those in need; and to assist bishops and priests in the proclamation of the Gospel and the administration of the sacraments.

Q. What is the duty of all Christians?

A. The duty of all Christians is to follow Christ; to come together week by week for corporate worship; and to work, pray, and give for the spread of the kingdom of God.[1]

From the Baptismal Liturgy...

The Presentation and Examination

Question   Do you renounce Satan and all the spiritual forces of wickedness that rebel against God?

---

1. Book of Common Prayer, 855–56.

Answer   I renounce them.

Question   Do you renounce the evil powers of this world which corrupt and destroy the creatures of God?

Answer   I renounce them.

Question   Do you renounce all sinful desires that draw you from the love of God?

Answer   I renounce them.

Question   Do you turn to Jesus Christ and accept him as your Savior?

Answer   I do.

Question   Do you put your whole trust in his grace and love?

Answer   I do.

Question   Do you promise to follow and obey him as your Lord?

Answer   I do.

The Baptismal Covenant

Celebrant Will you continue in the apostles' teaching and fellowship, in the breaking of bread, and in the prayers?

People   I will, with God's help.

Celebrant Will you persevere in resisting evil, and, whenever you fall into sin, repent and return to the Lord?

People   I will, with God's help.

Celebrant Will you proclaim by word and example the Good New of God in Christ?

People   I will, with God's help.

Celebrant Will you seek and serve Christ in all persons, loving your neighbor as yourself?

People   I will, with God's help.

Celebrant Will you strive for justice and peace among all people, and respect the dignity of every human being?

People   I will, with God's help.[2]

Thanksgiving over the Water

The Celebrant blesses the water, first saying

> The Lord be with you.

People   And also with you.

Celebrant Let us give thanks to the Lord.

People   It is right to give him thanks and praise.

Celebrant

We thank you, Almighty God, for the gift of water. Over it the Holy Spirit moved in the beginning of creation. Through it you led the children of Israel out of their bondage in Egypt into the land of promise. In it your Son Jesus received the baptism of John and was anointed by the Holy Spirit as the Messiah, the Christ, to lead us, through his death and resurrection, from the bondage of sin into everlasting life.

We thank you, Father, for the water of Baptism. In it we are buried with Christ in his death. By it we share in his resurrection. Through it we are reborn by the Holy Spirit.

---

2. Book of Common Prayer, 302–5.

Therefore in joyful obedience to your Son, we bring into his fellowship those who come to him in faith, baptizing them in the Name of the Father, and of the Son, and of the Holy Spirit.

At the following words, the Celebrant touches the water

Now sanctify this water, we pray you, by the power of your Holy Spirit, that those who here are cleansed from sin and born again may continue for ever in the risen life of Jesus Christ our Savior.

To him, to you, and to the Holy Spirit, be all honor and glory, now and for ever. *Amen.*[3]

◆

All this reeks of hospitality. How can the church possibly take responsibility for the ills that maim and destroy God's children? The task is overwhelming. It's hopeless, except that gestures of hospitality work magic! Whenever one of us is willing to make the caring, welcoming, or sharing gesture, others find the courage to join in.

Holy hospitality is the essence of the ministry that belongs to the Body of Christ. When we set aside the nonessentials, faithfulness is simply making sure that all God's creatures are fed, clothed, nurtured — in short — living the abundant life God promises.

The eucharist, then, is the ritual expression of the patterns of ministry that identify Christians in the world. It is only when we approach worship from this vantage point that we are able to keep before us the ministry to which we are called.

---

3. Book of Common Prayer, 306–7.

The multisensory quality of liturgy, Recovering a tribal sensibility

HUMAN EXPERIENCE AS A TEACHING TOOL

Catholics[4] are incarnational Christians. We believe that God is among us, and that in God's presence, we are working to realize God's Realm in our world and in our lives. If the work of Christ's Body in the world has to do with feeding and being fed, if it has to do with righting wrongs and healing brokenness, then the focus of catholic context on symbol and image makes perfect sense. Worship must be tactile. It is about sensing God's presence, not just thinking about it.

Worship, in a catholic (or if you will, eucharistic) context, is all about seeing, hearing, feeling, smelling, and tasting God's presence in God's world. All the senses are available to grasp the impact of the gospel — the teaching of Jesus — on the lives we live, day by day. What follows is framed around the assumption that the experience of worship engages all the senses.

The world of science fiction suggests that the evolution of the human animal is toward a state in which being is purely intellectual. Everyone has seen bad movies whose characters have rudimentary bodies barely able to support heads containing huge and powerful brains. As we imagine the evolution of Christian practice and theology from the early church, through the sixteenth-century Reformation,

---

4. The term "catholic" might be difficult for some. It is not my intent to refer to the denomination whose headquarters is in Rome, but rather, to any community of faith whose life is characterized by a sacramental system serving God's mission to restore the dignity of all creation. One might be tempted to skip over the possibility of discomfort, but it seems essential to think of the church as a single body rather than as its many denominational expressions. For this writer, the term "catholic" maintains that focus.

a movement toward a more cerebral expression of the faith is obvious. If one looks across the denominational (and nondenominational) landscape, one sees expressions of the faith ranging from truly incarnational (sacramental) to utterly cerebral (confessional) patterns.

In recent years, aboriginal Christian communities have worked toward an understanding of what it means to worship in the cultural context of a Native community. *The Chant of Life: Inculturation and the People of the Land* describes the issues involved for aboriginal communities in the Episcopal Church.[5] The experience of aboriginal people is interesting to consider because their heritage demands that they live in the context of close relationship with the earth. They do not, in fact *cannot*, separate cerebral, theoretical reflections about life from the living of it in real time and in a real place.

The work of establishing justice in the world is a daunting task. Faithful Christians are continually tempted to rationalize an escape from that charge. It is easy to articulate reasons for avoiding social responsibility, but when one is face to face with hunger, homelessness, or injustice, it is difficult not to respond.

Spirituality is a natural and essential part of human existence and thus is an important aspect of the life of the church. But it is essential that spiritual practice be balanced with a commitment to ministries of peace and justice in the world. Engaging the senses helps to create a balance between piety and ministry. As we taste, hear, smell, see, feel the world we inhabit and as we move around in it, we are reminded that we are creatures. When we engage the senses

---

5. Mark L. MacDonald, ed., *The Chant of Life: Inculturation and the People of the Land* (New York: Church Publishing, 2003).

in worship — with incense, bread, wine, fabric, an embrace, music, and solemn procession — we are reminded that we are God's creatures and that we are called to live as one Body in God's creation.

And the daunting prospect of being Christ's Body in the world brings us back to the theme of hospitality. The beginning of the journey toward wholeness in creation is encounter with the other. When we put ourselves in the presence of need, our hearts melt, rationalization fails. And so the boundaries of our liturgical communities need to be permeable. It must be possible for all sorts and conditions of human life to gather around the table. When we "go . . . into the main streets, and invite everyone [we] find to the wedding banquet" (Matt. 22:9), the community re-creates itself in a new and transformative way. It becomes the wholeness it seeks to proclaim.

The Sunday morning worship experience is filled with opportunities to make gestures of welcome and hospitality. Those who serve as ushers and greeters, members of the altar guild, acolytes and eucharistic ministers, singers and instrumentalists, composers and poets are all in positions of high visibility. Their ministries on behalf of the congregation can signal either an atmosphere of exclusivity and control, or an attitude of welcome, inclusivity, and abundance.

The chapters that follow will reflect on the qualities of hospitality that should characterize liturgical ministries. I hope that reflecting about how people serving in these roles behave will awaken our sensitivities to the effect our behavior has, especially on the newcomers and strangers that visit our congregations.

Part Two

Liturgical Hospitality

Setting a Place at the Table for All God's Children

Inculturation
PRAYING CLOSER TO THE GROUND

The word "inculturation" has become more common in conversations about liturgy, as Christians whose first language
or culture is not English or Euro-American consider the place
of their cultural heritage in the arena of worship. For these
communities, questions about the relationship between religion and culture are important. When they came into the
Episcopal Church, mostly in the nineteenth century, they
were taught to leave their aboriginal customs outside the
door when they entered the church. But as leadership in these
communities has become indigenous and as they take a new
look at their cultural heritage, the possibility of re-integrating
church and native culture emerges. The journeys of African
American, Latino, Asian, and Native American Christians in
their involvement with Christian liturgy is not the topic of
this inquiry, but a word about inculturation is important.

Anscar Chupungco, OSB, defines inculturation:

> The core of the liturgy is a supracultural reality which
> the church received through apostolic preaching and
> preserves intact in every time and place. What incul-
> turation means is that worship assimilates the people's
> language, ritual, and symbolic patterns. In this way
> they are able to claim and own the liturgical core they
> received through the apostolic preaching. Today we
> have come to regard both the process of inculturation
> and the claiming of the Christian message by the people
> as an imperative to evangelization.[1]

---

1. Anscar Chupungco, *Progress and Tradition* (Washington, D.C.: Pastoral Press,
1994), 2.

The point is that liturgy is shaped by the culture in which it is prayed. American Christians often assume that the liturgical sensibilities common to mainstream American Christianity are appropriately expressive of American culture, but in fact, when we enter a church on Sunday morning to say our prayers, we most likely move into a world that has little in common with the rest of life.

Juan Oliver, priest, scholar, and educator, makes the point in very ordinary terms:

> In our excitement about the inculturation of the liturgy in African-American, Hispanic, Asian, and Native American communities, we have not focused similar attention on our Anglo experience of worship. Rather, we have assumed that American Anglo worship is already inculturated, although our Anglo worship is by and large a creature from another culture — nineteenth-century Britain.[2]

The habit of Episcopalians whose experience is outside of typical American expression has much to teach us. It is very useful to move among Christians whose culture demands that spiritual issues play out in the same arena as the rest of life. Perhaps the church at large can learn something here.

In order to create a worship experience that coaxes the newcomer into the room, there must be constant points of connection between the world of church and the world of work, pleasure, family, and friends. Making those connections is not always easy, but the journey is rewarding.

In the pages that follow, a variety of liturgical circumstances will be reviewed. As you read through these pages,

---

2. Juan M. C. Oliver, "Our Place: Inculturating [Anglo] Liturgical Space," in *The Chant of Life,* ed. MacDonald, 101.

think about the way in which you move through the moments of your life outside of the liturgy. What draws you in? What repels you? Try to apply the values that regulate your relationship with the world of grocery stores, banks, offices, and shopping malls to the issues of praying together.

The liturgical space and its setting
THE BUILDING ALWAYS WINS

It is not difficult to sketch the typical Episcopal church, in terms of its physical appearance. Certainly, there is architectural variety to be noted in building design and property use. One might note that there are some Episcopal church buildings that reflect a colonial understanding of liturgical space (box pews and triple-decker pulpits, for example) and some that represent late twentieth-century design concepts (freestanding altar, for example), but most fall more or less into the Gothic Revival mold. Thus, one expects to come off the street into a parking lot and to find a central entrance leading into a lobby-like space that is at least somewhat distinct from the main room. The room in which the congregation gathers is rectangular and filled with fixed benches facing the "front" of the space. The front of the room is divided from the seating area by a railing, behind which is a dominating altar and seating for vested folks. There is another dominant place from which the word is proclaimed. Or, there may be two desks, between which the reading and proclaiming of the Word is divided in some way. A baptismal font is probably evident, but probably not at this "east" end of the space. If the font designed as part

35

of the original structure is literally in another place, there may be a second font visible near the altar and pulpit.

Issues around the design and use of liturgical space that relate to liturgical hospitality fall into two categories. The space described above has significant implications for the congregation worshiping there. It is a room that gathers vested people in one space, not-vested people in another. What sort of church does this suggest? It divides the community into two classes of people in a way that fails to reflect the ecclesiology of the Book of Common Prayer. The implication is that the people on the altar side of the rail are presenting something that is received by those on the other side. This is not what the church says it believes.

The Book of Common Prayer says clearly that the mission of the church is to restore unity in creation and dignity among all God's creatures. This is the task of the baptized members of the Body. Clergy are set aside by the community to facilitate this task. The neo-Gothic liturgical space puts the clergy in the dominant role and relegates the baptized to a place from which they consume the ministrations of the clergy.

From the point of view of the visitor, the message is probably even clearer. One arrives as if coming into a theater or auditorium. The narthex provides a safe place in which one can made a decision about what to do next. If it seems better to back away, that can happen. Once inside, one takes a seat to await whatever comes next.

Architectural challenges are difficult to face. Buildings are expensive. If they are well executed, they have a significant permanence. If well designed, they are much loved.

The essential point to keep in mind in planning liturgy that is reflective of the baptismal covenant is that the building always wins. Human beings are sensate creatures. We read the space and respond. So a congregation worshiping in a building that doesn't accommodate itself to the eucharistic feast, as a reflection of God's intention that all God's people deserve to be nurtured, has an enormous task to engage in.

Furniture moving is not an easy thing to do. For one thing, it's hard work. But, if a worship space needs to change in order for the gospel to be clearly proclaimed, some opportunity for experiment is essential. Sitting in a space and talking about how it might be changed is ineffective. An architectural space is a physical thing. Being in the space is a physical experience. To understand what it would be like to worship in a setting where everyone sees the faces of others, one has to engage in the experience.

Retreats and conferences offer an opportunity for experiment. Planning an event in a facility that lacks a chapel provides the opportunity to create an alternative to the neo-Gothic norm. Allowing folks the opportunity to participate in the design of an alternative space is a powerful experience.

One hears stories about congregational experience in situations where a beloved worship space is suddenly unavailable. Perhaps there has been a fire, or maybe a major renovation project is undertaken. The event, whatever it is, forces the community to gather somewhere else, perhaps in a parish hall. Of course, there is grumbling and anxiety at the outset, but not infrequently the forced move takes on a transformative tone, especially if the resident liturgical planners have the foresight and courage to use the opportunity for experiment. "I was nervous when I came into the room and saw the table in the middle of a half circle of chairs, but I like looking at others as I pray!" "Standing in a circle to receive the sacrament felt good."

Welcome

THE CHURCH'S FUTURE MEMBERS ARE OUTSIDE
THE COMMUNITY

Some years ago, I served a small congregation as interim rector for most of a year. The congregation had been a vital suburban parish, but the neighborhood, as often happens, changed over time. What had been a white, middle-class community was becoming a primarily black and Hispanic neighborhood. The congregation had not caught up with the shifting cultural reality.

The church's buildings occupied a corner lot, the church at the intersection, and a fellowship, office, and education building was toward the center of the block. At the end of the property opposite the church was a large parking lot. Approach to the church for Sunday morning was achieved by car. People drove to the intersection and turned in front of the buildings. One had to know where the parking lot was, because there was no sign, and the interruption in the tall hedge along the sidewalk wasn't visible until one was passing the drive.

Parishioners parked their cars and entered the buildings through a back door. One walked down the hall, past the chapel, and into the kitchen, where a pot of coffee was ready. Mostly, folks arrived there a bit before service time to drink coffee and perhaps smoke a cigarette. The cue to enter the sanctuary was the beginning of the organ prelude. Entrance was down the hall and into the church through a door under the pulpit. After the eucharist, the folks went back to the kitchen to socialize and say good-bye.

After one or two Sundays, it occurred to me that I hadn't seen anyone come thorough the "front" door at the back of the nave. At the end of the service that Sunday, I tried the door. It was locked. I encountered an usher who said, "Oh, we don't bother unlocking it on Sunday. Everyone comes in through the kitchen."

Welcoming people to the Sunday morning experience requires the occasional assessment of congregational habit. When we become familiar with the buildings, habits, and patterns of congregational life, we forget how difficult it was to discover how things work. Developing and maintaining an atmosphere of welcome takes constant vigilance.

Periodically, congregational leaders should assess parish habit. Perhaps this list of questions might spark additional thoughts about the particular behaviors that should be evaluated.

- Will people know how to arrive and enter the building?

- What will be expected as they come into the space?

- Is finding a seat a self-evident experience, or does getting settled require instruction?

- Will newcomers know how to handle books and service leaflets?

- What happens to children?

- Where are the bathrooms?

Decorum has been highly valued in Episcopal circles. Decency and order are prized characteristics. As cultural diversity alters the way communities understand decency and order, the look, feel, and sound of the assembly changes, but there is always a quiet sense of discomfort among Episcopalians if things seem a bit too loose. This tradition sometimes interrupts the flow of hospitality. For example, most Episcopalians recoil at the thought of a presider giving verbal directions during the service. Folks are expected to know what comes next. "That's what inquirers' classes are for!"

In order to proclaim the gospel, the church needs to attract people to hear the proclamation. Without a pervasive sense of welcome, folks won't come. It is essential that the community adopt an attitude that assumes people don't know what to expect. Seasoned parishioners simply must accommodate to the need for a clear sense of welcome in the course of the Sunday morning liturgy.

An aura of abundance
IF FEEDING THE HUNGRY IS THE CHURCH'S TASK,
MORE IS NEVER ENOUGH

The cook who has the responsibility of feeding a family or community on a regular basis quickly gets a sense of how much food to buy. People are fairly predictable in the amount of food they consume. One gets into the habit of sensing what is necessary. Thus, the question of having enough on the table to provide those gathered with a satisfying meal is not an issue.

It is not so when the congregation gathers to eat and drink in a sociable, hospitable ambience. Who knows how many people will show up? How long will people want to linger?

Do they arrive with the expectation of munching politely on a symbolic morsel or do they expect to be fed? What if someone is genuinely hungry?

The conviction that we can feed the hungry rests on the assumption that God really does set a table in the wilderness. Without faith that food for the hungry is at hand, the commitment to serve withers. If our eucharistic gatherings are ritualized representations of the call to feed, then our gatherings must express the quality of abundance.

We have all ended a Sunday morning in the parish hall with an insufficient supply of stale doughnuts, an urn of barely drinkable coffee, and a plate asking for donations to cover the expense. If our worship experience is to represent our commitment to service, we must do better.

The interpretation of the feeding of the multitude with which we began this inquiry hinted at a human instinct that is useful here. We are, at heart, hospitable. At home, we mostly understand the need to provide abundantly. Everyone likes to "put on the dog" when company comes. One way to make the connection between the religious life and the life of service in and to the world is to pull our entertaining instincts into the worship experience. It takes time, because the spiritual side of human consciousness has been formed to resist excess. We're not sure that it's okay to party in church. But when the community is given the opportunity to fold a luncheon experience into the eucharistic celebration, the hesitation we have on Sunday morning to *really* celebrate will vanish. Of course, the prayer attendant to this issue is the constant hope that one Sunday morning, a starving street person will wander in and get fed.

Accessibility

Making certain that the places in which the church gathers and the activities the church sponsors are accessible is always a challenge. Every human being on the planet lives with particular skills, abilities, and perspectives. Sometimes it is impossible for a person with one particular set of resources to appreciate the circumstance of someone with a different set.

Assumptions about accessibility are rather like the assumptions about welcome described a few paragraphs earlier. People tend to be blind to their blindness.

The first and obvious issue is physical approach. If the worship space is at the top of a flight of stairs, a significant number of people in the community won't be able to worship. It's not just the person bound to a wheelchair who will be affected, but anyone who walks with difficulty. If receiving the sacrament requires another climb, the physically challenged person will be excluded twice in the same experience.

If we see the accommodation of the excluded person as an exception to the rule, the sense of exclusion may be heightened. I recall a Sunday morning in a congregation I served that had ceased using the east-end altar in a typical cruciform building in favor of a freestanding table in an open space at the crossing. The congregation gathered at the west end of the nave for the Service of the Word, then at the Peace moved to stand around the table. One member of the congregation had been confined to a wheelchair for years. She was accustomed to waiting patiently at the bottom of the chancel steps for the eucharistic ministers to serve those gathered at the rail, after which they would come to her with bread and wine.

As communion was served in the new configuration, one could not miss the glow on her face. For the first Sunday in a long time, she received the sacrament alongside her family and friends.

One way to ease the tension between uniformity and accommodation in the variety of physical abilities people bring to the worship experience is to encourage a variety of postures in the course of the liturgy. If some people are kneeling, some standing, some sitting, at a particular moment in the liturgy, those unable to stand or kneel will not feel excluded.

It has been typical for Americans to think of people living in nuclear family structures: Mom, Dad, 2.5 children. For decades, since the mid-1950s, television promoted this vision. It has never been as pervasive as people might assume, but the family construct is a pervasive image, even though TV sitcoms have broadened the imagery in prime time. People who live in a traditional family structure are likely blind to the degree to which they project their lifestyle onto people who don't share their circumstance. It is useful to examine the way events are advertised and planned with sensitivity to the reality that people live in families, marriages without children, partnerships with children, partnerships without children, monastic institutions, and as single persons. People in all these situations deserve to feel welcomed.

The early conversations among a small group of parish clergy that precipitated the development of the current

Prayer Book began with conversations about who should be present at the eucharistic table. These clergy were convinced that the entire community, including children, needed to be present.

Much work has been done over the past few years to realize this dream. In some places, the liturgy has been expanded to include an experience especially for the kids. The children's sermon is an example of such an inclusion. In other places, rites specially designed for children and their parents have been created. In other places, the children have been included, not as a special class of humanity, but as equals. I visited a congregation in which a twelve-year-old served as cantor. His peers joined him gleefully. One transept in the neo-Gothic space was free of furniture. It was a place where hyperkinetic children in stocking feet could run freely without making much noise, and in which infants could be walked during the sermon. When the congregation gathered around the freestanding altar, children were invited to dance to the hymnody. And perhaps most importantly, as the presider laid hands on bread and wine during the eucharistic prayer, all the children present, gathered immediately around her, were invited to touch the elements in blessing. I don't recall ever seeing a more potent moment of eucharistic devotion, not only for the presider and the children, but for the congregation as a whole.

Accessibility is an elusive but important issue. If the people we hope to invite into the church run into roadblocks, even invisible ones, they may never find their way in the door, much less become part of the community.

A special word about children
GATHERING ALL AGES AT THE TABLE

One of the hallmarks of liturgical renewal in the twentieth century, at least for those who pioneered the Book of Common Prayer, was the vision that the eucharistic celebration was less than complete unless all ages were present. The church has struggled to come to grips with what it means to create a multigenerational eucharistic aesthetic.

When we consider the issue of accessibility, it is essential to keep in mind that the eucharist, at its best, is a multigenerational event. Don't assume that children require a eucharistic celebration styled to their developmental needs. Instead, find ways to cope with their developmental limits in a gathering of the entire community.

Musical style
CULTURAL DIVERSITY CREATES A CHALLENGE

Twenty years ago it was not difficult to describe the music that would be used in a typical Sunday liturgy in the Episcopal Church. *The Hymnal 1982* was in the pews. The choral and organ repertoire was virtually all from northern European and American sources. Most church musicians working in congregations with a significant music program prided themselves in their ability to successfully imitate English cathedrals. The music was always sophisticated and in good taste. It is important to note, of course, that this typical Episcopal/Anglican model was not in place everywhere. One of the interesting statistical realities in the Episcopal

Church is that while the typical Episcopalian worships in a large congregation, the typical Episcopal congregation is quite small. Even so, where music flourished, in either an amateur or professional context, music in the style of the English cathedral was the model to copy.

Then, in 1993, the Office of Black Ministries at the Episcopal Church Center published *Lift Every Voice and Sing 2,* a collection of hymns and chants for the African American community within the Episcopal Church. To be sure, and as its title suggests, this was not the first publication of music for use in the church apart from the English model. There have been hymnals in various Native American and Chinese communities since the nineteenth century. Small collections in Spanish have also been available for a considerable time. But *Lift Every Voice,* as a complete hymnal to be used by a black, mixed, or even a white suburban congregation moved the Episcopal Church beyond the assumption that the only musical resource required was a hymnal in the model of *The Hymnal 1982.*

Simultaneously, the use of instruments other than the organ began to appear. In some cases, pianos came into the worship space where a useable organ could not be afforded. In other places, jazz and rock bands found their way into Sunday morning worship. Of course, in the 1960s the "folk mass" found use as a means of keeping teenagers in church. The musical style of the folk mass wasn't really the musical style familiar to the teenage crowd of the period, but drums and guitars had a certain appeal.

The relationship between musical style and hospitality is complicated. It was noted above that in earlier times it was not difficult to describe the musical style that characterized the liturgical activity of a particular denomination

46

and, within the denomination, the variants that could be expected. Since the last part of the twentieth century, however, people have been decreasingly interested in preserving a particular denominational or congregational style, especially if that maintenance is for the sake of maintaining traditional identity. Increasingly, young people, and presumably at least some newcomers, feel free to integrate the music they like. This freedom creates a picture in which much experimentation takes place, and enormous variety can be seen.

The conversation about musical style needs to occur in an atmosphere of openness. It is no longer useful to assume that the models of excellence from previous generations are the appropriate guide for the present and future. At the same time, it is important to retain a commitment to quality. In the same way that attention to the food and drink we serve reflects an aura of abundance, the music we listen to and sing should be the best we can afford.

Technology
ARE ANGLICANS ALLOWED TO BE COOL?

In 2005, Trinity Church in lower Manhattan installed a digital organ in its worship space to serve as an interim instrument while the congregation deals with the task of replacing the pipe organ that was destroyed during the attack on the World Trade Center in 2001. Two responses to this rather shocking event echoed within the musical community. Some were scandalized that a room filled with computers could be allowed to masquerade as a musical instrument. Others were amazed, if still discomforted by the experience of this computer-driven pretender because of the high quality of pipe-organ sound it produced.

In the first half of the twentieth century, it was rare for a congregation to read liturgical text and music from anything other than a bound volume containing official denominational resources. Today, through-composed leaflets containing everything the worshiper needs to read and sing are increasingly in use.

Projecting images (text, music, photography, graphics, art) in the worship space is slower to catch on than other technological advances, but it's becoming more popular.

The Internet provides the possibility of instant communication among any number of people situated in far corners of the globe. It provides, as well, the possibility of the instant delivery of digital files.

These and other advances that characterize the electronic culture we are moving into have vast implications for the way we worship and the means by which we prepare for worship.

I have written about this in two other places, and libraries about the relationship between technology and worship are rich.[3] The important thing to note about the use or avoidance of technology is an important topic for the liturgical planner. There are dangers at both ends of the spectrum. Refusing to pay attention to technological developments, in a cultural circumstance where finding what one wants is a stronger draw than denominational or congregational

---

3. Clayton Morris, "Prayer Book Revision or Liturgical Renewal? The Future of Liturgical Text," in *A Prayer Book for the 21st Century*, ed. R. A. Meyers, Liturgical Studies 3 (New York: Church Hymnal Corp., 1996), 241; "The Prayer Book in Cyberspace," in *The Oxford Guide to the Book of Common Prayer: A Worldwide Survey* (New York: Oxford University Press, 2006).

loyalty, is dangerous. Equally dangerous is the hope that technology can solve all problems or, for that matter, fill the church with newcomers.

Tradition

... BUT WE'VE ALWAYS DONE IT THAT WAY!

What is tradition? The word is usually used to identify an ancient characteristic a culture or institution wants to preserve. "Why do we do it that way? Because it's traditional." If one asks the typical Episcopalian to describe the worship space of a traditional church, it is likely that the description will be of a neo-Gothic space: cruciform in shape with nave, chancel, and apse. And yet, the typical church building in the period that preceded the arrival of Gothic architecture on the American scene is the colonial, box-pew building. The colonial space and the neo-Gothic space are opposites. The colonial space divides the room into boxes, assigned to families. The boxes are gathered around the double- or triple-decker pulpit. When the eucharist was celebrated, a table was brought into the center of the space. In the neo-Gothic space, the room is hierarchical and processional. One moves from street to narthex to nave, chancel, and sanctuary. One's rank in the community determines how close to the holiest place in the room one is allowed to go.

The biblical model for the eucharist is the supper Jesus and his friends ate on the last night they were together as a community. One imagines that the meal was eaten in a modest room. Seating was probably on cushions on the floor. Perhaps there was a low table to hold bread, wine, fish, nuts, whatever. Isn't this tradition? Why has the church chosen to name Gothic architecture as traditional when in fact its use is a recent innovation?

These thoughts about the word "tradition" appear here because the standard defense against innovation is the invocation of some notion of tradition. "It's just not done in the Episcopal Church!" One rejoinder from those urging the community forward into new ways of being is a serious look at history. In such an inquiry, one often discovers that the pattern of behavior, value, strategy, or form that is labeled tradition was in its time a more radical innovation than what came before. The point, simply, is that if we are to invoke tradition as the rationale for resisting change, we probably should notice that history is all about change, constant and continual change.

Aesthetics
WHOSE TASTE DOES WORSHIP REFLECT?

Episcopalians like to think that their worship is of the highest quality available. Doing things decently and in good order is a good thing. Choosing the best we have to offer and using it well is a good thing. It is essential, however, to put the value of quality into a cultural context. That which represents quality in one cultural circumstance might well be impossible to achieve in another context. That doesn't mean that one culture is superior to the other. It just means that two communities are different.

Music provides an example. Episcopal congregations are often drawn to the model of the golden age of English cathedral music as a goal to be achieved, even in situations where fewer than a hundred people gather for the primary liturgy on Sunday morning. Why would any worshiping community expect to produce musical performances requiring a large ensemble of professionally trained and compensated musicians in a circumstance where the volunteer choir numbers seven on a good weekend?

The value of quality in liturgy is essential, but it has to do with creating the best offering out of what is available and authentic. Whether the issue is music, vesture, architecture, style, movement, or any other component of the liturgical experience, achieving an aura of quality doesn't have anything to do with misappropriating something from outside the community.

Several years ago, the Associated Parishes Council spent Sunday morning with a community of Native Christians on a reservation in northern British Columbia.[4] The morning was divided into two activities. The council members arrived as a young, Anglo, female priest was preparing for the eucharist. We took places at the front of the nave, and as we waited for the service to begin, we noticed that six or seven parishioners, all Native, filed into the back rows of the pews. The eucharist proceeded in a pattern that was perfectly familiar, except for the text of the eucharistic prayer, which had been crafted to use local imagery, notably the image of the migrating salmon. Those of us at the front of the nave participated with energy. Those at the back mostly sat quietly.

---

4. The Associated Parishes Council for Liturgy in Mission was founded in 1946 by a group of Episcopal priests who were concerned about worship. Their work was one of the most potent forces in the development of what was to become the 1979 Book of Common Prayer. The council, a group of about thirty people, meets annually to consider a topic of interest to the church in the field of worship.

When the liturgy was over, we all moved next door into the parish hall. There we found a dozen or so Natives who had avoided the liturgy, some because they were women preparing the feast that would be our lunch, others because they did not feel called to participate in an Anglican eucharist.

As the afternoon came to an end, and we drove off, having said good-bye to our new friends, I realized that our experience in the parish hall had far more liturgical, spiritual, *and* aesthetical integrity than what we did in church.

This brief reflection raises many questions, but I think the point is clear. Just because a text, architectural setting, vestment, song, or pattern of movement is in a book, or represents a long-standing use, or seems attractive, doesn't make it aesthetically appropriate.

Accommodation

JUST LET IT BE

I can't count the times I've found myself visiting a church, appreciating the building. There is something begging to be changed. Perhaps it's the placement of the altar or the arrangement of seating. Whatever the issue, my host's response is often something like, "Well, yes. It would be good to do that. But it would take an enormous sales job to convince the older folks, and . . . well . . . it doesn't really matter, after all. It's the thought that counts."

No! It *does* matter! At several other places in this text, the notion that the nonverbal *information* we encounter in worship speaks volumes is underscored. Here it is important just to remind ourselves of the principle. We are multi-sensory beings. Just because we aren't consciously aware of communication that we are absorbing doesn't mean we aren't taking it in. And more importantly, we can be sure that negative information, in the form of an inappropriate architectural setting, for example, is being processed and is affecting the way we behave.

An awareness of *liturgical hospitality* is an essential tool in the planning of the liturgical life of a congregation. Without attention to the way in which worship affects, changes, supports, and repels those who come to the table, we will never greet the newcomers we need among us to continue the work we have to do in the world. With that awareness and a willingness to put hospitable practices into use, the community will be transformed into a thriving manifestation of Christ's Body in the world.

Part Three

Liturgical Ministries

Setting God's Table for the Feast of the Kingdom

In the previous section of this book, theological foundations and principles that shape the worship life of a community were discussed. In this section, we will look at a variety of liturgical ministries that combine to create the worship experience.

The personality of a congregation is a combination of a vast constellation of small moments, a combination of the points of view, attitudes, and habits of everyone who is active in the community. All the behavioral details of the bustle of congregational life combine to create the identity, purpose, and quality of the organization. Thus, a congregation will do well to notice the details of behavior that combine to inform the visitor or newcomer of what it's about.

The pages that follow are an attempt to draw attention to the details that combine to create the worship experience of a congregation's ongoing life. Because every congregation is unique in its local circumstance, culture, and habit, these descriptions are incomplete. But perhaps they are sufficiently suggestive to remind the reader of missing pieces.

The important things to bear in mind are several:

- No detail is unimportant.
- Nothing should be left to chance.
- Taking time to evaluate liturgical behavior is always worth the effort.
- Including advice from people not connected to the worshiping community is often revealing in helpful ways.

It is, perhaps, surprising to realize how many specific tasks combine to create a worship experience. To understand the way in which worship comes to be in the community, all these moments of planning and execution, large and small, need to be taken into account.

Behind-the-scenes staff
EVEN ACTIVITY IN THE BACK ROOM MATTERS

Regardless of the size of a congregation or the complexity of its physical plant, somewhere in the structure of community life are the people who close up the building on Saturday afternoon after preparations for what will happen on Sunday are complete. The assumptions that support the work of behind-the-scenes folk communicate their commitment to hospitality, or the lack thereof.

Describing the backstage functions we have in mind here in a single stroke is difficult because of the diversity of staffing strategies employed by congregations. Large and maybe even medium-sized congregations often employ staff, full-time or part-time. Smaller congregations mostly rely on volunteers. In the smallest congregations, some of these functions might not exist at all. With that caveat in mind, here are some examples.

Administrative assistance
HOSPITALITY IN PRINT, ON THE PHONE, AT THE OFFICE

Congregations require some level of administrative support. In a small congregation, the tasks of Sunday leaflet preparation, correspondence, and record-keeping might be accomplished by the pastor, but whoever does the work should have hospitality in mind. With every task, the question of accessibility should be asked. Is a printed document self-evident, or does decoding it demand prior experience? Does an announcement of a congregational event contain enough information to attract the newcomer, or does it assume that the potential attendee was around last year and the year before that? If the congregation has a Web site, does it communicate in an open, self evident way?

Pictures are an important tool in the search for ways to express welcome and hospitality. The parish pictorial directory is useful to newcomers attempting to learn people's names. Pictures of members of the congregation on a bulletin board in the hallway serve the same purpose. Pictures of congregational activities provide a sense of what life is like in the community. Of course, pictures on the Web page are attractive, communicative, and descriptive of parish life.

What about the message on the answering machine? Does it communicate clearly in an accessible way? It is tempting to load the opening greeting with details about the weekly service schedule, what to do if there is an emergency, directions to the church, and other hospitable data. What does that do to the caller who simply wants to leave a message?

If complex answering systems and Web site development seem intimidating and expensive, ask for help from members of the congregation. Most of the time, a parishioner with technical expertise and maybe even equipment to donate can bridge the technological gap.

A primary issue for the person who manages congregational communication, whether in print or spoken announcement, is the problem of jargon. We all use shorthand when we communicate with family and friends. People who live together for a long time communicate in partial sentences using a code that develops over time. Sometimes, they finish each other's incomplete verbal articulations automatically. Similar evolution is likely to characterize communication in congregational life. As communities live and work together, transparency in communication is taken for granted.

I am reminded of my first season as rector of a small congregation in a farming community. The first major event in that season was the annual Christmas bazaar. It was one of the highlights of the social season in the town. It had two elements: a bazaar stocked with holiday food, crafts, and gift items, all suitable for wrapping up and giving to friends and neighbors. On Friday, lunch was served, and it was simply understood that everyone in the small business community would show up to enjoy the feast.

The town had a half-dozen Christian congregations and a fairly rapid turnover in clergy. It was common for folks to indulge their curiosity about new clergy by doing a bit of church shopping in the first few weeks after a new arrival. That had happened when I arrived, and as a result, there were a few newcomers in the process of getting their lives folded into the life of the congregation as preparations were being made for the Christmas bazaar. Wednesday mornings there was a simple eucharist, followed by typical altar guild work. I was eager for a particular Wednesday morning when I had learned that women of the parish planned to meet after the eucharist to make plans for the Christmas bazaar. I told the new women about the meeting and urged them to attend. I was pleased at what I assumed would be the thankful and congratulatory response of the old timers, as they noted the presence of new helpers. We celebrated the eucharist, made our way into the parish hall, poured coffee, and sat down.

To my horror, the bazaar chair called the meeting to order, rattled off a few code phrases, pointed to particular women, and adjourned the meeting. The newcomers had been utterly ignored.

The women of the parish had not intentionally ignored the newcomers. They simply hadn't entertained the idea of intentional welcome. I had quiet conversations with a couple of the bazaar veterans, and the new folks found their way into the circle. And, I hope, a lesson about the need to be continually aware of the need to welcome was learned.

The idea of perpetual, ongoing attention to welcome is as important in the print medium as it is in oral communication. Even for the regular church attendee, attention to the accessibility of written and printed materials is important. Anyone accustomed to receiving mailings on a weekly or monthly basis from the same source comes eventually to anticipate and largely ignore the mailings. "Oh, that again!" Thus, if there is a change in service schedule from spring to summer, the announcement might not be received. Finding new ways to attract the receiver's attention is essential.

As is the case with any institutional routine, from time to time the work of the parish communicator should be challenged, not to question the communicator's competence but to make sure that the communication and the assumptions standing behind the communications strategy are fresh. Just as the recipient of a routine mailing grows complacent over time, so might the preparer of these documents fall into a static pattern that is less than it might be.

The Sunday morning leaflet
IT'S ALL ABOUT THE VISITOR

The Sunday morning leaflet can be an invitation to the visitor or newcomer, or it can be a gnostic document accessible only to those who have become accustomed to its format. As we think through the variety of issues that determine whether or not the Sunday morning eucharistic gathering is an event connecting the worshiping community to the world and the church's ministry there, attention must be paid to this important, ongoing project.

Increasingly, congregations are creating leaflets that contain all the text, music, and rubrical cues the worshiper needs in the course of the liturgy. This is an expensive and time-consuming task, but the result is a very useful tool. Especially for the newcomer or visitor, the opportunity to turn one page after the other to encounter everything necessary is a clear gesture of hospitality. As the church office becomes more high-tech, resources are being made available to facilitate the preparation of attractive leaflets.[1]

Beyond the sense in which this style of service leaflet is kind to the visitor, having all the material in one place makes it possible for the liturgical planner to shape worship habits in some very specific ways. For example, if one hopes the congregation will attend to the eucharistic prayer by watching the presider rather than following the text, leaving the body of text articulated by the presider out of the leaflet encourages the congregation to look up. Instructions about movement or posture fall easily into place. Photographic or

---

1. For example, *The Rite Brain 2004, The Rite Light, The Rite Song 1.5,* and *The Rite Word 2004* can be ordered from Church Publishing: *www.churchpublishing.org.*

artistic images can be included in the leaflet to underscore the homiletical intention of the day or season.

It should be noted that transcribing text and music into a weekly leaflet is a task requiring visual sensitivity and care. A page turn in the middle of a hymn will decrease the liveliness of congregational participation. The temptation to reduce the size of a musical score to fit it easily on the page may produce an image that many find impossible to read. Using a combination of paper and ink color that results in low contrast will make reading difficult, especially in low light (at the Easter Vigil, for example). Red ink on beige paper is a bad idea!

Another caution: it is the responsibility of reprinters of copyrighted material to seek permission and to document permission given at the point of insertion. Over the past few years, churches and dioceses have faced serious legal action with devastating financial implications as a result of ignoring this responsibility.

Another advantage of printing a fully comprehensive leaflet is that it allows the liturgy and music planners to choose resources from a wide range of possibilities. Instead of passing out copies of a special hymnal on occasion, or worse, limiting choice to those available in *The Hymnal 1982*, choices can be made from the increasing broad spectrum of materials that are available. The range of materials available includes eight volumes available from Church Publishing,[2] along with excellent resources from other denominations.

Liturgical planners (and bishops) are sometimes confused about what resources may legitimately be used in Sunday morning worship. *The Hymnal 1982* is the official

---

2. *El Himnario, Enriching Our Music 1, 2,* and *3, The Hymnal 1982, Lift Every Voice and Sing, Voices Found, Wonder Love and Praise.*

hymnal of the Episcopal Church. It was approved by General Convention of the Episcopal Church after a thorough theological review of the texts. Thus it automatically meets the expectation of the rubric on page 14 of the Book of Common Prayer.[3] There are valuable materials commended by General Convention available from Church Publishing that are increasingly used on Sunday morning.[4] It should be noted as well that legislation approved at the last several General Conventions has encouraged liturgical planners and musicians to look for materials beyond the borders of the Episcopal Church for new music, particularly in the context of liturgical planning that attempts to be responsive to specific inculturative needs. Presumably, authorization for the use of such materials falls under the responsibility of the priest ministering in a congregation to supervise the musical ministry of the congregation (and delegate responsibility for its management to the musician).[5]

The task of leaflet production is enormously simplified by the application of technology, but for some, the leap from a simple, one-sheet-folded leaflet to a booklet seems intimidating. Again, it is useful to seek the help of people in the community who have made the transition to technology in their personal or business lives.

---

3. "Hymns referred to in the rubrics of this Book are to be understood as those authorized by this Church. The words of anthems are to be from Holy Scripture, or from this Book, or from texts congruent with them."

4. *Lift Every Voice and Sing 2; Wonder, Love and Praise; El Himnario; Voices Found; Enriching Our Music 1, 2, and 3.*

5. Canon II.5: "It shall be the duty of every Member of the Clergy to see that music is used as an offering for the glory of God and as a help to the people in their worship in accordance with the Book of Common Prayer and as authorized by the rubrics or by the General Convention of this Church. To this end the Member of the Clergy shall have final authority in the administration of matters pertaining to music. In fulfilling this responsibility the Member of the Clergy shall seek assistance from persons skilled in music. Together they shall see that music is appropriate to the context in which it is used."

Building maintenance

WOULD YOU KEEP HOUSE LIKE THIS AT HOME?

Too often churches have a characteristic musty smell. I'm not speaking here of the lingering aroma of incense or burning candle wax, but that dank odor of damp dust and collected debris. Not infrequently parish halls become the storage place for boxes of old Christmas pageant costumes and broken Sunday school furniture. The kitchen is stocked with cast-off implements, china, and silverware from dozens of former rummage sales.

Surveying a church property in this condition makes one wonder why Christians put up with conditions at church they would never allow at home. What is it about church life that makes shabby housekeeping acceptable?

Whatever the answer, the shabby surroundings of an ill-kept church do not communicate hospitality. No one wants to linger in an unkempt place where breathing the air is an unpleasant experience. Whether the work of maintenance is given to a professional or is managed by volunteers, congregational leadership must pay attention to the *look* of the rooms in which people are asked to gather.

This concern for well-kept space extends far beyond housekeeping issues:

- Is the light in classrooms sufficient to read by?
- Are the pianos scattered throughout the physical plant in tune?
- Can the congregation's audiovisual equipment be counted on to perform when it is rolled out of the closet?
- Is the kitchen's dishwashing equipment efficient enough to attract volunteers after the potluck supper has ended?

65

A special case in the maintenance department is the grounds in which the church is set. Some congregations are lucky enough to have a devoted volunteer who takes pride in the garden in its seasons. But if such an angel isn't available, it is still important to provide drivers-by with the impression that the congregation's home is loved and cared for.

This is another ongoing challenge in the life of a congregation that requires discipline. Think of the house in which you make your home. Is there art hanging on the walls? Think of a particular piece. Do you recall the last time you actually encountered it? As we grow accustomed to the spaces we occupy, we become accustomed to the way they look, feel, and smell. That does not mean, however, that the character of the space ceases to affect us. Think, for example, of a noisy appliance. I recall the heater/air conditioner in an apartment I occupied for three years. It was a wall unit that worked perfectly to maintain a comfortable temperature. But it was noisy, so noisy that if I was watching TV, I had trouble hearing dialogue while it was running. At first, I would grab the remote and adjust the volume, but as time went by, I got lazy. In time, I ignored the irritation, but if I stopped to think about it, I realized that the irritation was still there.

Sometimes, church buildings look drab because the community assumes that making them attractive is an expense the congregation can't afford. Import stores and fabric shops can provide inexpensive but attractive decorating details that will suggest that the congregation living in a church care about the quality of their life together.

Don't miss the opportunity, perhaps on the occasion of a visit from a stranger or newcomer, to assess the character of the buildings in which your congregation spends its time.

Childcare
WHAT DO FAMILIES NEED? WHAT DO THEY WANT?

The question of childcare has two distinct dimensions in congregational life.

We live in a world in which legal liability is an omnipresent issue. Churches must make certain their childcare facility meets the legal code and that the people who staff the center are certified to do so. There are simply no exceptions to this rule. Of course, in addition to the legal details to which the congregation must attend, it is important that a facility is attractive enough to welcome children and their parents.

This is a project that will especially interest families with young children. It should be noted that this is no longer solely the province of mothers. Dads are taking a more central role in the routine chores of childcare. Nor should it be assumed that a child has two parents. And it should not be assumed that the child's parents are male and female.

Increasingly, families prefer to attend church together as a family. In many places, Christian education classes are scheduled so as not to conflict with the primary worship service on Sunday. Whatever is offered in terms of childcare, ushers and greeters should not assume that infants belong in the childcare facility. Parents and families make that choice.

In dealing with the question of the Sunday morning schedule and whether educational opportunities should coincide with church as an adult event, congregations will do well to seriously explore the options. It is not just parents and children, in the context of family life, who benefit from sharing the Sunday morning worship experience. The congregation that worships with the entire age range of people in the community has a worship experience with a particular quality that is diminished when children are shunted off to another room.

I recall a recent visit to a cathedral congregation's mid-morning service organized especially to accommodate families with small children. I witnessed the children's delight in being incorporated into the service and also the delight on the faces of elders who were charmed by the obvious joy in the children's response.

The dinner party

IT WAS, AFTER ALL THE LAST *SUPPER!*

As we come to the center of the eucharistic celebration — the meal — we face some absolutely essential considerations. The historical models from which the eucharist derives are the Last Supper, the Passover, and the *chaburah,* a ritual meal that probably shaped the event we know as the Last Supper. These models were not polite rituals separated from the fabric of everyday life. They were meals, festive meals. They were moments in which the connection between life in the real world and spiritual contemplation and aspiration met.

On the night before he was crucified, Jesus begged his disciples to invest their lives in the act of feeding and being fed. He begged them to live and to share that life with whoever sat at table.

I wonder if anyone has done a serious investigation of the church potluck (or covered dish supper, in some places). If the study has been done, it would expose the scandal that Christians eat too much. But as we consider the eucharist, that indulgence is just what our Lord begged us to do. Come. Eat. No price. Enjoy. Live. The door is open. Come on in. You are welcome!

I spend much of my telephone time chatting with liturgical planners about issues and challenges. If I am stumped about how to advise, my textbook is usually my grandmother's dining room. My mother's parents lived in the center of the small town where I grew up. Grandma's door was always open, and her house was a place of hospitality. The convenience of its location, its proximity to school and my father's workplace, made it a place of gathering for siblings, cousins, parents, aunts, and uncles. One could always count on refreshment there.

There was nothing particularly interesting or exotic about Grandma's place. There were no magic formulae to appreciate. She simply understood that an essential part of her daily round was anticipating the arrival of guests. I imagine that there were nights when she grumbled under her breath as she put herself to bed. But for those of us who were the recipients of her care in providing a place to gather and be, her efforts were transforming.

I invoke the image of a hospitable dining room simply because it is the best guide I can imagine when questions about etiquette for the eucharistic table emerge. There is no better place to articulate the connection between our worship life and our life in the world than in the meal that draws us together as Christ's Body.

69

The altar guild

CAN THE KEEPERS OF THE HOLY GRAIL BE
WELCOMING?

A congregation's altar guild is probably the most conservative group in the constellation of liturgical task forces. They tend to be conservative, not necessarily in the political sense, but in the sense that they take responsibility for the conservation of the church's liturgical tradition and care for the treasures of vestments and vessels. This conservative role and the organizational identity it fosters create a serious problem.

The church, as an established institution, always struggles to maintain a balance between institutional stability and the need to maintain a discernable relationship to the world. Because the altar guild, by description, is a conservator of tradition, it is likely to err in the direction of stability. One is tempted to recall the old expression, "But we've never done *that* before."

Who serves on the altar guild? In earlier times, the answer was simple: a group of women intentionally appointed by the rector. The rector's intention, presumably, was to appoint women who were worthy to work inside the sanctuary, behind the altar rail. Another selector, operative in most congregations, had to do with the guild's schedule. Meetings and work sessions were mostly during the week and on Saturday morning. Thus, women who worked full time outside the home would be unlikely candidates. Of course, this model changed over the last half of the twentieth century, but it is important to note the exclusive nature of the organizational DNA of the model institution.

It may be helpful to note, as well, that the traditional role of the altar guild was to set tables and to care for the objects used, to arrange flowers and worry about a myriad of other housekeeping details common to the liturgical life of the congregation. Increasingly, the job description has changed. Take, for example, the liturgies of Holy Week and Easter. Will there be a procession through the streets on Palm Sunday? Will there be a simple meal tucked into the Maundy Thursday celebration? Who will construct the "life-sized" cross for the Good Friday veneration? What about an immersion font for the Easter Vigil? And then there's the lighting of the fire. And so on.

On another front, congregations are making their worship spaces more flexible. Sometimes this means simply unscrewing the pews so they can be pushed around. Sometimes it means constructing portable platforms for occasional use. Sometimes it means a total renovation of the church interior with the expectation that furniture is moved on a seasonal or occasional basis. Lighting, sound reinforcement, seasonal or occasional banners, and other decorations are becoming more important. These tasks can be managed in the congregation by setting up some sort of "stage crew" to work independently of the altar guild, but it is probably a better strategy, in the long run, to expand the work of the guild to include these functions, in order to avoid creating tension between opposing forces operating on a single playing field.

Holy hardware

THINK "DINING ROOM"

The typical container for eucharistic wine on Sunday morning is a silver goblet, considerably larger than one would expect to find on a dining table at home. If the congregation is able to afford it, the goblet is probably engraved and studded with jewels, real or imagined. It this the best cup for the eucharistic celebration? No. The secondary reference here shouldn't be to a baronial table or, worse, a reference that is entirely devoid of any connection to a common meal. The vessel in use should remind the congregation of occasions of feasting, people gathered around an abundantly laden table. Pottery is an alternative, in the sense that it lacks the suggestions of opulence or *churchiness*, but if pottery is the choice, it must be fired in such a way that it can be kept scrupulously clean. Glass is probably the best choice. It is simple. It can be as elegant as the budget allows. The wine contained in the cup can be seen. It is easily kept clean.

About cleanliness: one advantage to a silver chalice is that the chemical interaction between the alcohol in the wine and the precious metal maintains sterility. When other materials are used, care must be taken to insure that the vessels do not harbor contaminates. Carefully washed hard-surfaced materials, like glass, are ideal.

Increasingly, the bread of choice for the eucharist is not the previously ubiquitous wafer. The use of common bread is important because it reminds us of the dining room. The use of bread suggests that the shallow silver plate, with its ecclesial engraving, is less useful than it once was. Baskets lined with linen or a shallow glass bowl are a better alternative.

The choice of bread for the eucharistic feasts illustrates an essential point about the focus of the liturgical occasion. When bread is broken, when it has aroma, flavor, and texture, when there is a danger of crumbs falling to the floor, the experience is one of real life. The bread pulls the worshiper into an everyday context of common experience. And, more importantly, it puts the worshiper into a context in which the activity of the moment is feeding and being fed.

When the typical church supply house wafer is used, those palpable, human connections disappear. What fills the vacuum is a host of spiritual inventions about holiness: "The wafer should not be chewed. *All* the crumbs must be salvaged. Silence must accompany the reception of the Host." And so on.

If the eucharist is a sacramental expression of the ministry of the church in and to the world, it had better be table bread.

Napkins and tablecloths are, well, napkins and tablecloths. They should be useful for their purpose, easy to maintain, and simply elegant to look at. Many years ago, in San Francisco, Anna Crosley served as vestment maker to bishops of the Episcopal Diocese of California. She was fond of reminding those who would listen that the primary symbol associated with the chasuble is its shape, not its decoration. She hated vestments onto which representational decoration had been stitched. She made an important point. Why should a piece of cloth intended to clean the side of a cup be inscribed with a series of crosses? Do we really need to be reminded that we're engaged in a sacramental act? Do the crosses serve that purpose?

Our culture has taught us that the arena of the sacred stands apart from life in the usual sense. We move into

73

a sacred space that is purposefully set apart from the real world. In the context of that sensibility, images and vocabulary that have to be explained seem perfectly reasonable. But if our mission as Christ's Body in the world is to be in redemptive contact with the world, the sacred place and its images must be accessible to anyone who passes by. Once again, the issue is hospitality.

When the altar guild names the table service used for the eucharist, they speak of corporal, paten, chalice, and purificator. One imagines that most folks know what a chalice is. They've watched *Monty Python and the Holy Grail.* But can the average worshiper identify the other terms? Probably not. When we plan a dinner party at home, we speak of tablecloths, plates, goblets, and napkins. If the focus of our Sunday celebration is the sacramental expression of feeding and being fed, why would we use terms that avoid the connection between feasting and its ritual representation by veiling that connection in a recital of uncommon terms?

This question is one of many that need to be asked in the altar guild arena. Where the altar guild's identity is shaped by the need to preserve a set of procedural assumptions from the past, their presence will do more to repel visitors or newcomers than to invite them in.

Where does the instinct to function as conservator come from? Until the 1979 Book of Common Prayer introduced the church to the possibility of variation in liturgy, liturgy in the Episcopal Church was pretty static. Buildings were virtually identical, at least in plan. The Prayer Book rite was, well, the Prayer Book rite. Musical style varied slightly within the bounds of northern European and mostly English repertoire. Altar guild manuals reflected a singular approach to the task of holy housekeeping.

If one is forced to choose a topic, a focus, for conversation about liturgy in the Episcopal Church at this moment in time, it is the question of diversity and orthodoxy. We have learned over the past decade or so that the Episcopal Church speaks Ojibwa, Japanese, Mandarin, French, Spanish, English, and a host of other languages. We worship in small and large communities. We are an urban, rural, and suburban church. We are young, and we are old. One could go on.

Taking these realities seriously is a huge undertaking. In addition to the weight of considering the complexity of the diversity of the church, there are questions of standards, authority, and orthodoxy. If each community is encouraged to adapt its liturgical practice to meet local need, how will the church continue to speak of the unity that is maintained by liturgical practice?

Changing the altar guild's approach to its task and, thus, its identity, won't provide an answer to this question, but helping the guild see its role in a more inclusive and invitational light will help the church find its way forward.

I have no empirical data to support this notion, but it seems likely. I imagine that the altar guild crowd who intentionally or unintentionally erect roadblocks between God's creatures and the sacraments behave in exactly the opposite mode when they entertain friends in their homes.

Vestments
WHAT *SHALL* WE WEAR?

This thought brings us to the question of vestments. Often, in terms of design and decoration, less is more. It is good, from time to time, for a Christian community to stand back and take a look at its liturgical practice. Ask questions: Why does the presider dress this way? The deacon? The choir? Can we articulate a rationale for the way folks dress up for eucharist? If we can't, it is unlikely that the congregation or visitors will read the costuming in a meaningful way. This is not to say that vestments are unnecessary, but that a conscious rationale for their use will help the community determine what to wear and how the vestment should be designed.

As you consider the question of vesture, don't be afraid to think outside the box. The typical red, green, white, and purple palette can be expanded. The custom of limiting vesture to these four colors by season is only one of many patterns that has characterized the liturgical life of the church. Even the shape and style of vestments can be adapted to meet the needs and desires of a local congregation. Experiment!

Don't limit your choices to vestments available in supply house catalogues. If you can afford it, find a local vestment maker to help you make choices and develop designs. If you have people in the congregation capable of working effectively with fabric, think about creating your own vestments, using a style, colors, and materials that are locally available and, if possible, unique to the region.

Ushers and greeters
WELCOMERS, NOT GATEKEEPERS

It's interesting to imagine a newcomer's first visit to a church. How does a Sunday morning fall into place for a family of four? What happens to a single person or a young couple who decide to visit a church for the first time? What goes through the mind of a bride who isn't going to church when she confronts the task of finding a place to host her wedding? Is it the ad in the Saturday paper that provides the necessary introductory information? Is it the *look* of the physical plant one drives by on the way to work in the morning? Is it the testimony of a friend, relative, or neighbor who happens to be a member of the congregation?

Whatever the case, the moment comes when the newcomer figures out how to park the car or how to get to church by public transportation and finds the courage to walk through the door. Let's talk about Sunday morning as a primary example of initial greeting.

The question of getting there is probably the first challenge. The challenge is different, depending on the physical and geographical circumstance. In an urban setting, the question is most likely the choices of public transportation available. In a rural or small-town circumstance, driving directions and the availability of parking are the issues. The point is that folks need the information that will help them arrive safely and on time.

Once people have arrived at the parish property, questions of getting into the building emerge. Is the route from the parked car into the worship space self-evident and accessible? Can one see how to approach the building? Does the path accommodate canes, crutches, walkers, and wheelchairs? Is the entrance inviting? Will the newcomer feel welcomed in the attempt to find a place to sit? All these are questions the congregation should ask of itself.

If there are challenges that cannot be immediately corrected, people can help. If the front door sticks, someone should be assigned the task of being there to help, at least until the problem can be repaired.

What happens when newcomers arrive with children? Increasingly, families are put off by the insistence that the children be sent to another place. Even if the "other place" is Sunday school, parents may prefer to attend church as a family. The congregation should be prepared to welcome those who arrive.

Ushers can be welcoming greeters or gatekeepers. The gatekeeping usher is one who assumes that the people arriving for worship know where they are and what is expected. It's possible, as well, that the gatekeeping usher has a preconceived notion of who should be coming through the door. For example, in a congregation that prides itself on the superior quality of its choral music and preaching, children may not be expected. They make noise.

The welcoming greeter is one who is alert to the conditions that might be disquieting to someone attempting to enter the space. This usher will be on guard to sense what can be done to make the person coming through the door feel at home.

Lest we be tempted to demonize gatekeepers, it should be noted that habits that develop in liturgical circumstances grow over time. Regular attenders of a particular church develop common patterns. The people who take on tasks like passing out leaflets at the door absorb those patterns. Perhaps in a congregation whose population is stable, the prospect of a newcomer or visitor simply evaporates. Folks forget that someone approaching might need assistance.

This thought suggests that the role of the usher is one that needs to be reinvented at least once a year. The people serving in this capacity need to be constantly reminded that they might be the agent of miraculous healing. They might be the agent through which a hungry soul is fed. They might be the reason hopelessness turns to joy.

Acolytes and servers
GIVE THEM RESPONSIBILITY AND AUTHORITY,
BE MULTIGENERATIONAL

At some point in my career as a parish priest, I noticed an interesting pattern in the behavior of people attracted to the ordained ministry. They would volunteer for roles within the Sunday liturgy in a particular succession. They would show up as ushers. Then after a time, one would see them in the role of reader. Then, perhaps, they could be seen leading the intercessions. Then, in some role, they would don an alb, perhaps as acolyte or eucharistic minister. Just before they announced their sensation of a call to ordained ministry, they could be found in the subdiaconal role (nonexistent in Anglican polity), standing next to the rector behind the altar.

We like to think of our Anglican polity as a system that has abandoned the old Roman model of ordination to minor orders, eventually resulting in priesthood, but we are still tempted to see the role of acolyte as having an ordinational quality. We need to be careful here. In any organizational circumstance, people who take on a role and play it faithfully and skillfully will become, to some degree, professional. What we need to guard against is a tacit sensibility that there are two kinds of people in the room, vested folks who are ordained and ... well ... something like that. Then there are the folks in street clothes who receive the ministrations of the vested ones. The question is: How do we encourage good performance from servers and acolytes without encouraging the dichotomization of the community that is already encouraged in places where the vested folks are separated from the not-vested folks by the altar rail?

Earlier in this text, I spoke about the eucharist as dinner party. That image plays well here, in a consideration of the role of acolytes and servers. Is the primary eucharist in the life of the congregation a formal affair, with uniformed waiter, responding to congregational needs in a choreography ordered decades before? Or, is it a relaxed gathering in which the guests play the role of waiter? Or, is it somewhere in between?

In a eucharistic gathering that is struggling to shift the imagery from the hierarchical model in which the one to be served is the presider toward one in which it is the presider who plays the role of server, the role of the acolyte will change. Perhaps the use of vestments will change. I was in a congregation recently where the use of vestments has been abandoned altogether. I don't know that this experiment works, but thinking about the acolyting role in terms of costume might provide some interesting new insights.

The role of the acolyte in the liturgy serves as a great lab for thinking through the quality of hospitality the liturgy expresses. Acolytes and servers who have memorized a complex set of choreographic rules and who are expected to follow them exactly will project an aura of studied formality. Acolytes and servers who are encouraged to be quietly and gracefully helpful as the banquet is served will project an aura of warmth and welcome.

Eucharistic ministers

Serving a meal with grace and a sense of welcome

I recall a moment in the life of a congregation I once served. The furniture had just been rearranged so that the people came from their seats to gather around the altar at the time of the offertory. They stood two or three deep in a circle around the table during the eucharistic prayer and to receive communion. The customary that was in use called for one acolyte, as the bread was broken at the end of the eucharistic prayer, to move toward the table where extra plates and cups were waiting. The extra plates and cups were brought to the altar to be filled. I think it was the third week in this new configuration that the acolyte given this task went to the table only to discover the cups and plates were not there. Why? Because the congregation was now standing around the altar in such a way that the task of moving plates and cups from one place to another didn't require the assistance of a vested server. Someone noticed that it was time to distribute bread and wine and the deed was done without ceremony.

This story suggests the need to think about how the choreography of the liturgy must change as liturgical style and assumptions evolve. For the most part, our assumptions about the role of the eucharistic minister were shaped in a hierarchically ordered neo-Gothic space. The eucharistic ministers, in that physical setting, had been invited into the holier space east of the altar rail and had an almost or-dinational identity and function. In a circumstance like the one I just described, the function of distributing bread and wine takes on a very different tone.

In the typical ecclesial ambience of an earlier time, the eucharistic minister participated in the act of protecting holy things from desecration. As I recall my initiation into the Episcopal Church in the early 1960s, I am reminded that one was expected to hold the wafer on the tongue until it dissolved. No chewing. The introduction of leavened bread has demonstrated another sensibility, but it is likely that the people charged with distribution have not changed their habit. How often do we see a lovely, ample loaf of bread in a basket and the eucharistic minister picking off minuscule bits to serve? At the end of the distribution, most of the loaf is still in the basket. Or how often do we experience the reception of the cup as a tug of war with the minister?

None of this is meant to deny that the reception of the sacrament is a holy moment. Rather, the intention is to argue for ceremonial that matches the emerging mood of the liturgy. As we rediscover that sense in which the eucharist is a ritualized reminder of our duty to feed the hungry and celebrate community around a festive table, it seems appropriate that the most important moment of active participation in the rite be one of profound human interaction.

Musicians

WHAT *IS* SACRED MUSIC, ANYWAY?

It's difficult to generalize about music in church because of the enormous variety of congregational circumstances that exist across the church. Episcopal churches are large, medium, small, and tiny in size. The availability of professional musicians, sometimes determined by economics, sometimes by location, creates another level of variety. Style varies from place to place, and occasionally a prejudice for or against the use of professional musicians determines the musical flavor of the weekly eucharistic gathering.

Music in worship can be divided into two categories: music sung by the assembly and music performed for the assembly to hear.

Congregational music making is a fundamental liturgical need. While congregations usually have at least one eucharistic celebration that doesn't include music, liturgy wants to be sung. Sung liturgy should be the norm.

What should be sung? Anglican liturgical form combines two great musical traditions: the singing of hymns by the congregation and the performance of musical settings of the eucharistic chants. The two distinct musical repertoires are combined in a variety of ways in congregational usage. In some places, the choir plays the primary role. In others, choirs do not exist. In a few places, the eucharistic music is performed by the choir, with the congregation standing in silence. In most places, congregational settings of the eucharistic music are sung by the people, and hymns are inserted at various points in the liturgy. Congregational singing is a corporate activity that requires a sense of community for success. Thus, an abundance of singing in the course of the liturgy will serve as a continual reminder that the Christian enterprise is something people do in community.

In addition to that symbolism, the physicality of singing adds an element of tactile liveliness that sitting or standing quietly to see and hear can't match. There is something undeniably positive about the experience of making music in community that belongs in the worship experience.

 This book is not about the details of congregational music making, but it is worth noting a few factors that contribute to the accessibility of music. There are some essential considerations about the singing of hymns, psalms, canticles, and eucharistic music that will make the difference between self-conscious music making and confident congregational singing.

Perhaps the most important factor is *acoustics.* We like to sing in rooms where we can hear one another. The good acoustical environment is encouraging, and, of course, a live acoustic improves the sounds we make. While it is true that improving the acoustic of a dead room can be difficult, sometimes it's just a matter of finding the courage to rip up the carpet. Where a dead acoustic is hampering the music-making ability of a congregation, an assessment of the problem and suggestion of solutions is an exercise worth engaging in.

Selecting repertoire can be a sticky business. Most congregations and their music leaders have a sense of what works in the community. Even where a community is comfortable with its musical repertoire, it's worth wondering, from time to time, whether the musical offering is hospitable and welcoming. This is not to say that music should be chosen simply to attract the curious, but that the music program in the congregation, along with everything else that happens week by week, should be challenged from time to time, just for the sake of seeing the program as an outsider would.

Where choristers and instrumentalists are available to perform music for the congregation to hear, the music must be understood to participate in the proclamation of the gospel. There is no need to entertain the congregation with a musical offering. If choral and instrumental music doesn't preach, it should not be included in the rite.

There is an important principle here. Musicians know that combining music with text creates a richness of meaning in which the text is interpreted. This fact suggests both caution and opportunity. The opportunity is that music performed within the liturgical rite will participate in the homiletical aspects of the liturgy. The caution is that this suggests the absolute necessity of preacher and musician to be engaged in ongoing dialogue about seasons and lectionary. It's not a happy thing when the offertory anthem contradicts the sermon!

Relating choral and even instrumental music to the homiletical content of the eucharist suggests a rethinking of placement of performed music in the liturgy. Should the congregation be asked to sit through an offertory anthem that goes on for six or seven minutes after the table is set? Would an offering from the choir as a prelude do more to set the tone for a particular liturgy than an instrumental piece?

Even more to the point, why not expect the choir, other ensembles, or soloists to read and preach? The choir library most likely has many choral settings of biblical texts that come up in the course of the liturgical year. Hearing a familiar biblical text set to music is a wonderful and meaning-giving event. Even in the reading of the gospel, where rubrics demand a deacon or priest as reader, it seems reasonable, on occasion, to have the deacon or priest announce the reading and then to step aside as the choir sings.

There are vast possibilities available to the worshiping community in combining text read to be heard, text read by the congregation or by parts of the gathered community, music listened to, music sung. Looking for interesting new possibilities will hold the community's attention.

Those who lead prayer and song
WHO CALLS THE TUNE?

As the Episcopal Church began to explore its current Prayer Book in the last quarter of the last century, priests and musicians began to realize that the basic patterns of worship and planning assumptions were about to be challenged. When trial use in anticipation of a new book began in the late 1960s, the 1928 Prayer Book had been in place for over four decades. Moreover, the ethos expressed by the 1928 Prayer Book had remained largely unchanged for more than four hundred years. Thus the experience of a new liturgical text provided an atmosphere in which liturgy, in general, could be considered in new ways.

For example, the experience of contemporary English raised questions about musical style. If we are going to worship in the language of the street, instead of the rarefied language of King James and Shakespeare, what musical style should characterize congregational song? If the new text suggests a more participatory role for the congregation, what other opportunities for involvement might the congregation imagine? If the new text expresses the eucharistic

86

vision in a more intimate way, how might the furniture be arranged to underscore that shift?

Those old enough to look back on the "good old days" of worship with the 1928 Book of Common Prayer will recall that there were no serious decisions to be made on a week-to-week basis, apart from the crafting of a sermon and the selection of congregational, choral, and organ music. Of course, questions of what vestments to use, how to arrange flowers, and other particular details were ongoing, but the structure of the eucharistic event and assumptions about how worshipers approached it were pretty standard.

At the same time that the 1979 book found its way into the life of the church, Episcopalians realized that its liturgical style might be of interest to people not born into the denomination. As the demographics of neighborhoods changed, the use of languages other than English in the liturgical context began to emerge.

In a variety of ways, these shifts in the relationship of the church to the culture in which it sits have created a new dynamic in the arena of liturgical planning. It is no longer possible for priest and musician to do their planning in isolation, simply fitting their contributions into a static structure and set of assumptions. This new dynamic, which has been with us since at least the last quarter of the twentieth century, has created a significant level of tension in the relationship between musician and priest, not infrequently resulting in the loss of jobs, especially for the musician.

The canons are clear. In the Episcopal Church, the priest in charge is responsible for the management of the liturgical enterprise, with the understanding that music planning is delegated to the musician. Raising the issue of this important relationship between two primary leaders in the worshiping community in the context of this inquiry serves as a reminder that the context in which the relationship is likely to thrive in a healthy way is the context of hospitality.

Liturgical planning must always put the questions of accessibility and hospitality in a place of primary importance. It is never enough to assume that the way we did it last season is the best way forward.

Movement

DANCING? IN CHURCH?

Congregational song is a community-building exercise. When the gathering makes music successfully, everyone has the experience of being drawn into something beyond themselves. The entire room full of people takes the same breath and exhales complementary sounds.

Congregational dance provides an even more intense experience of being The Body. A line of people, moving from place to place in a common step, each worshiper with a hand on the shoulder of another, creates a visual and physical experience of commonality. As participants sense the rhythm of the dance, settle into a pattern of relaxed forward movement, and slowly become comfortable with the exercise, the borders of physical, bodily sensation expand. It is no longer me, moving between the person in front and another behind. I experience the hand on my shoulder from behind, and the shoulder of the person in front. For a moment, we're tugging at one another, but then there is a sense of one body, moving in simultaneous, fluid unity. In this mode, congregational dance becomes an icon of community.

This writer isn't sufficiently skilled to articulate principles for the development of movement in worship, but there are others who are.[6]

Caterers
PREPARING A MEAL CAN BE COMPLICATED

The role of food in worship was discussed earlier, but in the specific context of the roles people play in liturgy, more needs to be articulated. To borrow a thought from the section on housekeeping, why is it that people will consume food in church that they wouldn't let anywhere near their kitchens or dining rooms at home? Bad coffee and stale donuts don't reflect hospitality and welcome.

To be sure, providing food and drink that is interesting, delectable, and of high quality requires energy, skill, and money. But if we want our liturgical expression to communicate a sense of abundance, joy, and celebration, we have to extend that intention to the provision of food. Perhaps a reference to the current coffee craze is illustrative. People who routinely pay three to five dollars for a cup of coffee on the street are unlikely to enjoy a cup of weak, tepid brew on Sunday morning.

Most communities have among them people who enjoy being in the kitchen and find fulfillment in entertaining friends and neighbors. The trick is to organize that enthusiasm and energy in a way that can provide a predictable flow of food and drink on occasions when the community gathers.

---

6. For more information and resources, log on to *http://www.saintgregorys.org.*

One of the most important aspects of planning what happens with food at the end of the eucharistic liturgy is the way in which the food is served. When the hospitality time is located in a place apart from the worship space, people must decide to go there. They make a conscious choice to attend what is a separate event because of its location. If it is possible, it is a good thing for the post-eucharistic social gathering to happen in the worship space, even as a continuation of the liturgy. It may even be possible to use the altar upon which bread and wine were blessed to hold some or all of the post-eucharistic food. Doing this makes clear the relationship between our life of prayer and our life in the world beyond the liturgy.

Some congregations are able to provide a budget to ease the process. In some congregations, it will be acceptable to expect people to contribute a modest amount. In other places, teamwork will make hospitality possible. Whatever the scheme, the welcoming congregation is one that takes this part of the weekly gathering seriously.

Rethinking the roles we play in worship
Giving up control

Each of the possibilities raised in these pages is likely to challenge ongoing patterns of behavior in the life of a congregation. We are people of habit. We develop ways of making things work, and we stick to them. People provide leadership because they enjoy doing the work, and challenges to positions of leadership are often greeted with a lack of interest or even disdain.

The lay and ordained pastoral leadership of a congregation, working out issues of inclusivity and hospitality, will do well to focus some attention on the question of how we play the roles we assume as leaders in congregational life. As people are recruited to lead, part of the emerging contract between the new leader and the community should be an understanding that leadership and control aren't the same thing. Everything that happens, as a particular or ongoing event in the life of the community, needs to be understood as a provisional event. Assumptions must be understood as being always open to question.

With these examples of the various roles that get played out in the course of a worship service in mind, we move to a discussion of strategies that can be employed to make changes that will provide a congregation with a more hospitable ambience.

Part Four

Programmatic Strategies

Changing the Rules in Community

If you are still reading, it is likely that you have an interest in asking questions about hospitality in the context of worship. In the previous section, we identified some elements of congregational life and activity that need to be considered in order to create an atmosphere of enhanced hospitality and welcome. On the pages that follow, we will consider some strategies to create that enhancement. But first, there is an important roadblock that needs to be set aside.

Imagining change in congregational life
IF IT'S NOT BROKEN, DON'T FIX IT? IT'S BROKEN!

The most disabling feature of life in the church is religion. This seems a startling assertion at first glance, but a bit of refection bears it out. One imagines that religion has been a feature of human consciousness since the beginning of human sensibility. A being capable of imagining death is capable of considering the possibility of avoiding death. The idea of life after death is a reasonable response to the awareness of mortality. Examination of humankind's dealing with the fact of death makes it clear that the expectation of life in the next world has been a feature of human culture throughout the ages.

Of course, it's not just death that plagues us; there is also the question of responsibility. As thoughtful beings, we naturally think about the consequences of our actions. Thus, reflection about guilt and redemption comes easily into considerations of the consequences of life and death. The notion that a supreme being, standing apart from but involved with life as we experience it, is a logical extension of the consideration. And so humans in search of meaning are naturally drawn into religious reflection. We are easily captured by promises of eternity and freedom from guilt.

Religion is clearly a natural part of the human condition. But the teachings of Jesus, as recorded in scripture, don't put religion in the center of things. More often than not, Jesus, as an observant Jew, gets in trouble for misappropriating or ignoring the religious tradition he lived with. If we set aside the lens of spirituality to consider them, the patterns of Jesus' life are instructive. In his personal struggle to be in the world, the pious use of scripture, prayer, meditation, and reflection were all plainly visible. At the same time, when Jesus encountered injustice in the world as he moved about in it, religious rules and principles were secondary to the drive to seek justice.

The patterns of Jesus' life illustrate a balanced appropriation of religion. Jesus was clearly a human being bathed in the tensive process of finding meaning in life. Pious spirituality was an important way in which to engage life. At the same time, Jesus' sensitivity to the suffering and injustice he encountered was, in the last analysis, more important.

The baptismal covenant clearly identifies ministries of social justice in the world as the focus of the church's identity. Suggesting that religion is a roadblock in the church's attempt to minister is not to suggest that spirituality has no place in the life of the church. Rather, identifying religion as a dangerous component of life in the Christian community recognizes the danger of having issues of spirituality as the sole or even primary focus of congregational life.

The balance of piety and ministry in the life of a community very easily falls over into the spiritual arena. It is simply less threatening to imagine evil in one's soul to be corrected by attention to spiritual discipline than to head out into the world in search of a hungry mouth to feed. Thus, change in a congregation's habit, its behavioral tradition, will occasionally need to be addressed.

It is always dangerous to stereotype, but for the sake of argument let us consider the personalities of three distinct congregational types.

There are congregations that thrive on the work of ministry — thanks be to God! They are enthusiastic, probably easy-going, not easily ruffled. They don't indulge in gossip. They find creative ways to *strive for justice and peace among all people.* They pray, study scripture together, and worship in community. Congregational life is in healthy balance, with mission and ministry always in the spotlight.

There are other congregations that have allowed the balance between spirituality and ministry to tip in favor of spirituality. Perhaps this change has come so slowly, over such a period of time, that the community is unaware that life in the congregation has changed.

Then there are those congregations that organize their lives, even if unconsciously, in order to avoid the possibility of being infected by ministerial commitments. These are communities that tip the balance in the direction of piety because they are convinced that the purpose of the church is to validate their personal lives.

Encouraging change in a congregation is a tricky business. Organizations resist change, if for no other reason than the fact that routine is comfortable. Life naturally falls into patterns, and those patterns repeat themselves. And so perhaps the first principle in the consideration of changing the relationship of a congregation to the world in which it sits is that communities resent being told how to behave by an alien expert. Maybe the easiest way to precipitate resistance to change is to have someone throw a suggestion over the wall from the outside. Even the clergy serving in a congregation, who may think of themselves as belonging, are likely to be considered alien if they attempt to serve as change agent for the community.

On the other hand, if the lay leaders in the congregation experience conversion to a life of social justice, their witness can lead the congregation forward. A story comes to mind.

A congregation in a middle-sized suburban community had begun an intense adult catechumenal project and was eagerly exploring what it meant to be an agency for justice in the world. On a particular Sunday morning, the organist was in the middle of the postlude when two men approached, waiting patiently for the performance to come to an end. When it did, the parishioner introduced his new employee to the organist, asking whether it would be possible for the newcomer to use the organ for purposes of practice. The organist sent the pair off to coffee hour, promising to catch up to them. A few minutes later, the trio reconnected with coffee in hand. The organist handed a key to the visitor. "This opens the door into the back hall of the church. Enjoy."

The newcomer was stunned. "That's it?" he asked. "Sure," the organist replied. "Just keep an eye on the weekly schedule so that you don't arrive in the middle of something."

Over the next few weeks, the newcomer showed up to sing in the volunteer choir and was soon functioning as baritone section leader. As time passed, he announced to his new friends that he had been asked to serve as accompanist for a local gay men's glee club. Periodically, he would provide a few tickets to choir members to performances of the choir.

Time went by and a crisis loomed on the horizon of parish life. For many years, the congregation had managed a rummage sale. There was a large garage at the back of the parish property with a pop-up door. Folks from the town would bring their saleable cast-off clothing, appliances, toys, books, and other household items and off-load it into the building. At odd times during the week, volunteers, mostly retired folks, would arrive to sort and price the merchandise. Then, twice a year, the accumulation would be hauled out onto the parking lot for the sale. This project netted the parish about twenty thousand dollars a year.

The crisis came as the sorting and pricing crew found it increasingly difficult to do the work. The founders of the project, who were the most committed, were aging to the point that they were unable to participate. Younger folks had commitments that made participation difficult. It would be almost unthinkable to call it off. No one could figure out how to stop the never-ending supply of merchandise.

The newcomer — organist, singer, and vestryman — had a suggestion. There was a hospice nearby serving the end-of-life needs of AIDS patients. They were struggling to stay afloat financially. They would be happy to take on the rummage sale if they could use the proceeds to help them stay afloat. The vestry applauded the idea.

This story illustrates one way in which change can be instituted. The process was slow, organic, not given to harangues about responsibility. The conversion of the rummage sale to an agency for justice in the community happened because a newcomer was welcomed into the community.

Managing change will look a bit different in every circumstance. Before a congregation is expected to adopt a new way of thinking of itself and a new approach to its corporate life, it is essential to consider a constellation of questions:

- How are decisions made?

- By whom?

- Who decides whether new ideas are implemented?

- Are there important decision makers who aren't part of the visible leadership of the community?

Like water, liturgy must be a living, moving thing. Water, when it is not moving, stagnates. Unsavory things begin to grow in it. It becomes useless. So in worship, the rites we celebrate, the style in which they unfold, the particularities of our liturgical behavior all must have room to move, shift, and respond to changes in the community, the neighborhood, and the world. The thoughts that follow are suggested as ways in which the need to change can be considered in the life of the congregation.

Self-assessment
STRATEGIES FOR EVALUATING A CONGREGATION'S LITURGICAL LIFE

People and institutions are equally handicapped when it comes to seeing themselves clearly. Just as individuals rely on consultation to provide a self-assessing mirror from time to time, so congregations that wish to stay healthy and realize their potential for meaningful life have the same need. Whether personal self-assessment is achieved in relationship to a pastoral counselor, spouse, therapist, or patient friend, the need is to experience something of the way one is seen by others. That data simply cannot be gathered in isolation.

One of the important dynamics in the liturgical experience of a healthy congregation is that, apart from God, there is no audience. Indeed, there are congregations in which the clergy and choir, from their elevated seats in chancel and apse, perform for the benefit of the congregation past the rood screen, in the nave. But the community gathered around the altar, even if the articulation of anthem and sermon are important moments in the liturgy, have a sense of participating in an event that is experienced from within.

The good news about the absence of audience is that the experience is that of a body. It is like the experience of singing in a choral ensemble or even playing on a basketball team. The sensation from within the group has little to do with what might be observed from the outside. This is a bodily experience of community.

The problem with this interior sensation is that no one is monitoring from the outside. Thus, when the liturgical planners gather for a staff meeting to evaluate what happened last week and use that data to plan ahead, they are probably missing vital information. There are any number of ways to fill in this gap.

Professional consultants abound. Architects, designers, and acoustical engineers can evaluate the worship space. Artists can assist with the look of the interior. There are others who can help evaluate musical performance, the musical instruments in use, and sound systems. Those with expertise in group dynamics and process can look at the way the community relates to itself, its neighborhood, and the world.

Any of these professionals may be useful from time to time. It is probably worth noting that it is less stressful to anticipate this need before a crisis in community forces the encounter.

But another possibility exists for providing an ongoing stream of evaluative data about the way worship looks from the sidelines. If it is possible, those who play major leadership roles in the liturgy should have the occasional opportunity to worship with the congregation or, perhaps, take a bird's-eye look at the liturgy from a balcony. This exercise needs to include the rector. In places where the absence of multiple staffing makes this impossible, there might be occasions on which a guest presider or musician could help it to happen.

Another way to achieve this experience of an alternate view of worship for those who lead is for the leaders to take whatever opportunity they have to visit other churches. Not infrequently, seeing a particular twist of behavior in a strange place will resonate with familiar habit back home, either in an affirming or critical way.

Yet another possibility for ongoing critical input for liturgical planners can be provided by one or more congregational volunteers whose task is to attend liturgical planning sessions. These people would, of course, be regular attenders of the services they comment upon and should be chosen for their ability to do their work in a mature and nonthreatening way. This critic might do little more than respond to occasional questions like "How did it look (sound, feel) from where you were on Sunday?"

Self-evaluation is nothing more or less than a healthy reality check, something people and institutions need to stay healthy and forward looking.

The invitation to communion
WHO IS WELCOME AT THE TABLE?

In 1981, the Church of St. Gregory of Nyssa in San Francisco began the custom of inviting everyone present at the liturgy to receive communion, putting their practice at odds with the canonical definition of a communicant in the Episcopal Church[1] and with the standard for the reception of communion by non-Episcopalians concurred at the General Convention of 1979.[2] Both statements assume that recipients of the sacrament must be baptized.

The rationale St. Gregory's uses is that the ministry of Jesus was one of radical hospitality. Jesus illustrated his concern for the welfare of all God's children by inviting the wrong people to his table and by showing up at the tables of people who lacked status within the Jewish community. How better to live out his ministry than to invite all who come to the table to share in the feast?

It is beyond the scope of this book to sort out the controversy about whether or not the practice of open communion is appropriate, but it should be noted that St. Gregory's position has launched an international discussion on the topic,

---

1. Title I, Canon 17: Of Regulations Respecting the Laity.
2. Resolution A043.

and churches are joining St. Gregory's in inviting everyone present in the assembly to the table.

The question of who is welcome at the table is central to the larger question of hospitality because it focuses the issue of hospitality in a very specific way. Whether or not a congregation and its clergy are convinced that defying the custom of the church is appropriate, this question encourages the community to develop a profound sense of intentionality about planning worship.

In an earlier time, the Episcopal Church had an orderly sequence in which people moved through their experience of church. They were born and were baptized soon after. It is worth noting that the baptismal rite was not a part of the liturgical life of the ecclesial community. Rather it gathered family and friends with the priest at the font privately. If there was one, the public event was a party in celebration of the baptism.

In this cultural expression of church, the baptized child grew and at some point in mid-maturation was prepared for confirmation — a mature affirmation of the faith. In the first half of the twentieth century, the baptized child would receive the eucharist for the first time at confirmation. In the mid-1900s, the church began to explore the possibility of communicating baptized children when they took interest in receiving. In 1988,[3] the House of Bishops of the Episcopal Church affirmed the notion that all baptized Christians should receive, and the practice of communicating infants at their baptism began.

It is useful to remind ourselves of this cultural expression of initiation and membership because of the specificity

---

3. General Convention Resolution B012a.

and impermeability of its structure. It is the expression of a self-identified and specifically identifiable community, moving through time in a particular, predictable pattern of behavior.

Obviously, inviting just anyone to the table totally disrupts the stability of this structure. But eucharistic hospitality cannot thrive in a closed system. If the only people welcome at the table are the people already there, the church won't grow, nor will it be informed by the world in a way that will lead to new opportunities for mission and ministry.

Formation for hospitality
WELCOMING PEOPLE IS A LEARNED SKILL

It is natural to assume that welcoming people in a hospitable way is second nature. Perhaps in a home environment, where hospitable customs are passed from generation to generation, that is the case, but in a congregational circumstance, where a diverse community of people come together week by week and occasion by occasion, we can't take for granted that people know how to welcome.

When a stranger enters our living room, there is no question about the new arrival's identity. We don't know this person. That fact will have to be reconciled in order for a next step to be taken. Is the intruder asked to leave or invited to sit and enjoy refreshment? In the domestic circumstance, the presence of a stranger is impossible to miss. That is true, as well, for the very small congregation. In a community where everyone knows everyone, the newcomer stands out clearly. But in medium-sized or large congregations, identifying the stranger isn't so easy. Maybe this strange face is a regular at 8:00 a.m. It's a large room. Maybe I've just not seen this person before.

Unfortunately, our instinct is to assume that the person we don't recognize belongs to the community. And so we move on. To function in a mode of continual hospitality, we need to develop the comfort to find out why the face we see in church isn't familiar.

The same issue is just as critical in the arena of inclusivity. Periodically, it is important to ask the question "Who are we?" I am reminded of another story.

I once served a congregation in which the continual arrival of newcomers was significantly changing the leadership base in the community. One year, at the Sunday morning annual meeting, the balance tipped. When the election of vestry members was over, the newcomers significantly outnumbered the old-timers. On Monday morning, as I always did, I poured myself a cup of coffee and sat down across from the volunteer receptionist, a woman in her seventies. She looked distressed. "What's wrong?" I asked. "We have to have another election." she said. "Why?" I replied. "Those people that were elected to the vestry aren't parishioners," she said.

This wonderful, self-giving member of the community, who was among its founders, simply couldn't imagine that these people who were unknown to her were members of the community she had served for so long.

Whether the issue is newcomers, people of color, children, or members of another social class, an attitude of welcome will develop only when we take a clear and careful look at the folks around us.

Visitors who use the church property
AN OPEN DOOR IS AN EVANGELISTIC OPPORTUNITY

I was, for a time, rector in a small church in a central California ranching community. In the five years I served that congregation, new people were coming into the community, and so the integration of newcomers was a theme. I recall getting together with a group of adults intending to join the congregation. I was curious to know what had drawn them to the church. One said, "I drive by here every night on my way home. The lights are on always on."

A church campus buzzing with activity is an attractive feature in any community. People coming and going, children making the noise children are wont to make, cars in the parking lot. The bustle of activity communicates an aura of life and health.

Use of church property by organizations that contribute to the health of the community at large communicates the congregation's concern for health and well-being. Twelve-step programs, youth organizations, social opportunities for the elderly, groups concerned with issues of immigration and citizenship, musical organizations — there are a host of possibilities. Of course, a church will choose the number of sponsorships it can handle and make choices to match the passions of the worshiping community, but maximizing the use of the parish property for the good of the community is an important congregational project.

This use of congregational property — and the complications it brings to those who maintain the buildings and grounds, who schedule its use, and who worry about budgets — is not entirely a selfless gift from the congregation.

It is useful for people in the neighborhood not associated with the church to have a look inside. Welcoming the visitor in this ecclesiastically neutral way gives the potential seeker an opportunity to have a secret glimpse inside. It might be valuable to make strategic use of bulletin boards in the hallways and meeting rooms.

How often we pass a church building at almost any time aside from Sunday morning to find the doors locked, the lights off, and the parking lot empty. How much more interesting to drive by a bustling center of interesting activity.

The church in the world
ONE LAST THOUGHT ABOUT MISSION

Finally, it's about feeding *all* God's children. The way forward is to be found at the intersection of Christian service and worship. The Book of Common Prayer that defines the worship of the Episcopal Church and, thus, defines the church's place in the world, puts the eucharist at the center of its worship life and baptism in the center of the eucharist. This focus of attention of initiating newcomers so that they may join the church in its ongoing ministry of feeding and being fed says some very important things about the way we organize our life of corporate prayer.

All of the details about liturgical planning focus, in one way or another, on the sense of welcome, or absence of welcome, expressed in the life of the community. "Holy hospitality" must always be at the center of our strategic planning and become a congregational way of life.

A Workshop Model

Engaging congregational leaders in conversation about the proposals outlined in these pages is an important part of making changes in the worship life of a congregation. The rector's responsibility for determining the liturgical personality of a community is always worked out in relationship *with* the community, not in isolation from it. Encouraging folks to express their preferences and explore possibilities will dramatically increase the level of commitment they have to the process and will ease transition into a new way of worshiping.

Don't attempt to engage issues of importance without identifying a facilitator to plan and lead the event. The facilitator doesn't necessarily need to be a paid consultant, but remember, asking someone within the community to take on this task may not be fair. It's much easier for a disinterested outsider to guide a conversation in which the community has a huge investment than for one of the community to do the job. A liturgical leader from a neighboring congregation — either a pastor or a musician — with some sensitivity to group process might be a good choice for a facilitator.

Identify a Topic

As you notice aspects of the community's liturgical life needing attention, make a list of the things needing to be addressed. Perhaps a parish survey would serve this purpose. Or perhaps an open forum, gathering interested folk, would work. Ask worshipers what they value in the weekly eucharist. Ask them what they're not so fond of. Ask about preferences. This exercise might be done in print, distributed with the service leaflet, or included in the congregation's newsletter. Have a small team of two or three people collate the responses and spend time discerning the topical patterns that emerge.

Once it's chosen, take care in articulating the topic. Clarity will focus thought. Fuzziness will add confusion to the process. Consider how people involved in the conversation will respond. Plan carefully.

Work on new ideas one at a time. Choose a particular issue. If it is based on a congregational survey, you might decide to work on something that will create a low level of stress as a way of introducing a new process without controversy. Or you might choose to tackle the issue that is most urgent. Whatever the case, maintain a focus on the particular issue you have identified.

Be sure that the conversation always has in mind the outcomes that the proposed change or activity hopes for. Keep a goal on the table at all times. It is obvious that when a community has a common goal, cooperation is not difficult to achieve. Coming to agreement about direction will make it easier to negotiate details.

Choose People to Participate

It is probably best to limit the number of people involved in initial conversations. Make sure, whatever the size of the group, that it is representative of the community. Some of the participants should be congregational leaders, lay and ordained. Some should be parishioners who have a commitment to the life of the community but don't necessarily involve themselves in making decisions or managing things. Every age group, especially young people and children, should be involved. It would also be useful to have one or two people not engaged in the life of the congregation to participate, as a way of providing a reality check as the conversation moves forward.

Create a Safe Environment for the Conversation

Early in this book, we compared worshiping communities whose central focus is mission in and to the world with those whose focus is personal spirituality or piety. For people who rely on the weekly eucharist to provide themselves with a sense of spiritual well-being, changes in liturgical habit are threatening to contemplate. The social-justice folk will probably find it easier to imagine reorganizing the worship experience. Their sense of spiritual well-being is more likely to be achieved in their work in the world.

Whatever the case, it is important that people can come to these conversations feeling safe about the experience. This is where the work of a skillful facilitator can be very important. The facilitator will sense when boundaries are about to be crossed and steer the conversation back in a less threatening direction. The facilitator can also serve as a referee, gently managing the conversation so that people don't encounter one another in a way that damages relationships.

111

Make the Experience Interactive and Multisensory

I was engaged in a conversation about using technology in worship. Someone in the group kept talking about the need to explore something called "multisensory worship." I found the title confusing. Yes. Of course. Multisensory worship. We have eyes, ears, mouths, noses, and nerve endings. We see, hear, taste, smell, and touch. Worship cannot be anything other than a multisensory experience!

I'm thinking here, not so much about whether our worship experience is especially colorful, or whether incense is carried in procession. Rather, I'm reminding us that it is a good thing to involve our whole bodies in an inquiry about the ways in which we worship.

Imagine that you're sitting in your living room, with your partner. One of you says, "I'm tired of the way this room looks. Let's do something different." If the project moves forward, you're going to move furniture. Sure, you might draw a floor plan, but it's going to be more than talk. You will engage most, if not all, of your senses in the inquiry.

Experience, Reflection, Reflection

The comments just above, about multisensory realities, suggest a model for shaping conversation about liturgical change.

Experience first! The best way to engage a topic about worship is to begin with the experience. If the issue is liturgical space, walk around in it. If you're talking about congregational song, begin by singing. If the question is how to encourage the ushers to be welcoming, do some role-playing.

112

Beginning with something that involves the whole body and that puts you in the environment the conversation is meant to affect will shape the inquiry in a real, not theoretical, context. Starting with experience puts the practicalities of the circumstance on center stage.

What did the experience mean? Once the group has experienced what it wants to consider, it is useful to engage in theological reflection. Teasing out the meaning-giving aspects of the experience helps people to recognize the import of every gesture, action, or comment that contributes to the liturgical experience

How did we get here? Reflection about the history of the community comes last. If we begin there, the conversation will bog down in the old "but we've never done it this way before." Because we have used all our senses to experience the issue and have wondered about how the experience changes the meaning of what we do, the storytelling that will characterize the historical reflection is likely to be informative and, usually, helpful.

It is often the case that conflict about proposed changes in the life of a worshiping community isn't about the proposed change at all. Entering into carefully planned and facilitated conversation can move people through a process of discernment that will ease the fear and maybe even identify the misdirected anxiety that is the real source of conflict.

Let's take as an example a liturgical habit that has almost disappeared. It once was the custom, especially in churches fitted with sophisticated lighting systems, to dim the "house lights" and aim a spotlight at the pulpit just as the sermon began. One imagines that a small group of ushers, or maybe the same usher every week, had the responsibility for this task.

There comes a new rector who observes that this is a place of worship, not a theater. The sermon is not a speech delivered to a passive audience, but part of the dialogue between and among the worshipers in the room. So the rector proposes that no change in lighting occur at sermon time. In fact, to dramatize the point, she announces that for the next few Sundays, the sermon will be delivered from the center aisle.

Predictably, the usher or ushers in charge of dimming the lights will be furious. Is it because they put a high value on dimming the lights for the sermon? Probably not. The issue, most likely, is that the new rector has robbed them of a job they've been doing for decades.

Pastoral care and parish policy often get confused. One way to sort out these two aspects of congregational life is to be clear: we may not always get what we think we need in our relationship with the congregation, but we're always loved and respected as children of God. At the end of the day, that is the message that needs to be communicated, no matter what developmental strategies are in the air.

A Workshop Strategy

The particular circumstances of a congregation, along with the complexity of the topic to be processed, will dictate the workshop agenda that will work best. The notes that follow can be adapted to groups large and small, conversations simple and complex.

Duration

The opportunity for a community to engage conversation about particular liturgical strategies will require varying lengths of time:

- an evening
- an evening followed by a half or full day
- a day
- an entire weekend.

Sometime the need for a face-to-face conversation about an anticipated change involves little more than the expectation people have to be included in the process. If there is little disagreement about the proposal under consideration, an evening to describe the process and solicit input from those gathered may suffice.

If the project involves the remodeling of a physical plant or the rearrangement of the worship space, the need might be a complex process spread out over several meetings requiring weeks or months to complete.

Leadership

When a conversation about a proposal for the implementation of something new goes wrong, it is usually the result of <u>inadequate leadership</u>. It is essential that the process outlined below proceed in an orderly manner. These suggestions will be useful as a workshop is planned.

- Engage the services of a facilitator who is (if possible)
  - not a member of the community
  - someone with professional credentials
  - someone with credibility among the participants

- Be sure that the facilitator is clearly informed of
  - the proposal
  - its impact on the community
  - those who have a stake in the outcome
  - any other factors that might affect the way participants respond, even if those factors are not articulated

It won't always be possible for a community to approach a workshop with professional help. Where that is the case, it is still essential that the event be planned and led as carefully and intentionally as possible.

The Space

Think carefully about the furniture, the room, and the amenities within the space.

- Where are the restrooms?
- Will the space be comfortable?
  - Is it big enough?

– Does the furniture work?

– Is it warm or cool enough?

– Consider the question of access for people with mobility, hearing, or vision issues.

- Whenever possible, arrange people so that they are facing one another. In a conference room with chairs around a single table, this happens automatically. For a larger group, avoid the temptation to arrange the chairs in rows facing a lectern. Put the participants in a configuration that allows everyone to see everyone else.

There is nothing more irritating than being placed in a space that fails to accommodate the process. If participants in a workshop are expected to view images on a screen, every seat in the room must have a clear view of the screen. If audio is to be used, it must be easy to hear. If participants are asked to read, the light must be sufficient. If they are asked to write, a comfortable table or desk is essential.

If the physical arrangements are inadequate, the conversation will suffer.

Sequence

The order in which events take place in the course of a workshop should be thought through in advance.

- Begin with an informal time of gathering in a hospitable setting.

– Plan a means to have everyone introduced.

– Are name tags necessary, or are the participants well acquainted with each other?

- Provide some form of food and drink (in ample supply, attractively presented) for the gathering time.

- When everyone has gathered and had time to enjoy the hospitality, gather the group in the place where the meeting will take place.

  - Make immediate announcements about creature comfort issues.

    * Locate bathrooms.

    * Make announcements about how "creature comfort" breaks will be taken. Sometimes breaks are built into the agenda. Sometimes it works better for people to meet their needs individually.

    * Check to see if anyone has personal needs to be considered.

  - Unveil the agenda for the event, and make sure everyone has an opportunity to voice concerns about the way time will be spent.

- Design an exercise to get participants thinking about the topic. Here are a few examples:

  - In a small group, ask each participant to answer a question designed to get the group thinking about the topic.

  - In a larger group, divide participants into groups of two or three to discuss the topic.

  - Ask participants (in large or small groups, depending on attendance) to articulate their hopes (and perhaps fears) about the outcome of the conversation.

The Topic

Present the topic under consideration. This might involve:

- the architect, presenting a construction or renovation project
- the musician and priest, presenting a change in the Sunday morning worship schedule
- the Christian educator, soliciting parental input for a new education strategy

It is tempting to assume that this part of the workshop is a lecture presented for participants to hear passively. Increasingly, people expect to be drawn into the presentation from the beginning. If this part of the workshop begins with an opportunity for participants to participate actively, their attention to the topic will increase.

Response

This is the core of the event, during which participants are given the opportunity to express their concerns and their support for the project under consideration. Attention to detail is essential to assure a positive outcome.

- Organize a specific strategy for the conversation.
- Make sure everyone has an opportunity to speak.
- Make note of comments in such a way that everyone witnesses the recording.
- Avoid excursions into irrelevant, negative, or uncharted territory.

Adjournment

End the event in an aura of hospitality.

- Perhaps another offering of food and drink is appropriate.
- Make sure everyone's participation is appreciated.
- Remind the community that being in community is more important than the issues under consideration.
- End the event with a particular leave-taking exercise:

  - a prayer
  - a song
  - the passing of the Peace.